£3

TM.

Y35964

VEGETABLE
COOKERY

P. Maruška and L. Nodl

VEGETABLE COOKERY

Photographs by O. Davidová and S. Němec

HAMLYN

Designed and produced by Artia for
Hamlyn Publishing
Bridge House
London Road
Twickenham
Middlesex

Copyright © 1986 Artia, Prague
© 1986 This edition by Hamlyn Publishing, a division of
The Hamlyn Publishing Group Limited
Translated by Dana Hábová
Graphic design by Antonín Chmel

ISBN 0 600 32500 8
Printed in Czechoslovakia
3/99/47/51-01

Contents

Introduction

Vegetables are one of the basic foodstuffs in man's diet. They are the source of indispensable minerals, important vitamins, particularly vitamin C and carotenes (vitamin A), and important fibre. They contain a large quantity of water and, in general, few carbohydrates. In leaf and root vegetables, the water content amounts to about 90 per cent, but in many fruit-bearing species and in lettuce it represents up to 95 to 98 per cent. After adding the average 0.5–2 per cent of fibre, only 0.5–5 per cent are left for proteins, 0.5 per cent for fats and 1–10 per cent for sugars.

Vegetables contain varying amounts of protein — peas and beans being good sources. Vegetable proteins, however, do not provide all the amino acids found in 'first class' proteins such as meat, eggs and dairy produce and must therefore be complemented by one of these or a grain product such as rice, wholewheat bread, nuts or seeds.

Fats are almost entirely absent from vegetables. In root vegetables, sugars are represented mainly by saccharose, in other species by glucose and fructose. Vegetables also contain pectins, starch and fibre. In spite of the fact that pectins and fibrous material are not digested by our bodies, their significance lies in promoting healthy functioning of the intestines.

Almost all vegetables are important sources of potassium, particularly leaf vegetables, cauliflower, broccoli, cress, parsley and parsnips. Magnesium makes part of the green plant pigment, chlorophyll, and is found mainly in spinach, tomatoes, peas and kohlrabi. Iron is found in greatest concentration in horseradish, pumpkin and corn salad, then in green leafy vegetables such as lettuce, spinach, tomatoes, carrots and kohlrabi. Some species also contain calcium and phosphorus. Various trace elements are present in other vegetables — for example manganese, molybdenite, cobalt, copper, zinc, fluorine or iodine — and these elements have recently become the subject of medical research.

Organic acids give vegetables their pleasant taste. Some vegetables such as sorrel, rhubarb, spinach and beetroot have a higher content of oxalic acid which binds calcium in digestion. These vegetables should be served with calcium-rich foodstuffs such as milk, eggs or cheese.

In terms of vitamins, vegetables contain valuable quantities of vitamin C and vitamin A as well as a small quantity of vitamins B_1, B_2, B_6, vitamin E and vitamin K.

Green and red peppers, horseradish, cauliflower, Savoy cabbage and Brussels sprouts, red and white cabbage, asparagus, kohlrabi, peas and radishes are important sources of vitamin C. Carotenes (vitamin A) are found predominantly in carrots and tomatoes, lettuce, Savoy cabbage, peppers, peas and runner beans.

Some vegetables (such as horseradish, onion, garlic, tomatoes and white radish) contain antibiotically efficient substances called phytoncides. Substances affecting the taste and scent of dishes and stimulating digestion are present in many vegetables especially white radish, radishes, cress, onion, garlic and horseradish. Plant pigments are represented mainly by chlorophyll, red carotenes, yellow flavones and red-blue antocyanogenous pigments.

Cooking and preparing vegetables

When cooking vegetables, or serving them raw, certain rules should be observed to ensure the best taste and nutritional value.

1. Choose fresh, good quality vegetables and salad ingredients.

2. Buy vegetables in small quantities which can be consumed quickly as long storage leads to loss of important vitamins.

3. Wash vegetables in cold running water, always in one piece, before cutting up. With leaf vegetables wash each leaf separately.

4. Slice or grate vegetables just before use and do not leave standing in water for a long time before cooking.

5. Cook vegetables for the shortest time possible. Always put them into boiling water. Reserve the water for other dishes.

6. If possible, vegetable dishes should not be kept warm for a long time or re-heated.

7. An acidic dressing helps to preserve the vitamin content of raw salad ingredients.

8. Cook vegetables in covered pots. Try to avoid stirring to prevent oxidation. Some vegetables such as cabbage are first cooked without a lid to allow any ammonia to evaporate.

9. The dietetic value of other dishes can be enhanced by serving vegetables or a salad with the main course. Of course, vegetables themselves can form a main dish.

The ever increasing demands on energy consumption in modern man require a radical change in his diet. Cooked and raw vegetables should become an everyday item of our diet throughout the year. This book provides many practical ideas to enrich your repertoire of attractive and nutritious vegetable dishes.

Professor RNDr. Karel Halačka, M.D.

All recipes serve four unless otherwise indicated.

List of principal vegetables

ONION FAMILY

Chives

The green leaves of chives are not only a savoury seasoning, but also an important supplier of vitamin C. Chives also contain vitamins of the B group, vitamin A, and a large amount of calcium, phosphorus and sulphur.

Garlic

Garlic is an important kitchen vegetable. Mature bulbs, sliced or crushed, are used as a seasoning in a variety of dishes. Garlic is rich in vitamin A and in vitamins B and C. It also contains a small percentage of vitamins E and K, and many minerals.

Leek

Leek is related to onion but has a finer taste. Both the elongated, cylindrical, white bulbs and the green leaves are used. They are often served cooked, with white sauces or au gratin, but are also a useful addition to many casseroles, soups etc.

Leek contains less sugar and more proteins than onion, as well as vitamin C. It is rich in minerals — calcium, phosphorus, iron, sulphur and magnesium. It also contains essential oils which promote gastric function and consequently the appetite.

Onion

Onion is widely used in all forms — raw, boiled, .stewed, baked and fried. It keeps well. It has a broad scope of taste, from pungent to sweet and delicate. All species contain vitamins C, B_1, B_2, and the leaves are rich in vitamin A.

Shallot

This is a very delicate, sweetish, small onion. Its fine taste is especially suitable for delicate dishes, both hot and cold, where the more penetrating flavour of ordinary onion would be too strong. Shallots are often pickled in vinegar.

Spring onion

The whole young plant with leaves and half-ripe bulbs is used, usually raw, in salads, spreads or marinades. It is often used in Chinese stir-fry dishes.

ROOT VEGETABLES

Beetroot

Beetroots come in many shapes and sizes. The small globe-rooted ones are most popular in salads. The young, crisp leaves are rarely eaten but are in fact delicious and nutritious. Beetroot is most familiar served with a salad, boiled and sliced and dressed with a sharp vinegary dressing. This tends to mask its delicate flavour. It is also delicious served as a hot vegetable and as a basis for the famous soup, bortsch. Never peel beetroot before cooking as all the red juice will then ooze out into the cooking water.

Beetroot is rich in minerals, magnesium, potassium, phosphorus, iron, vitamin A, and in vitamins B_1, B_2 and C.

Carrot

A widespread and popular root vegetable of orange-red or occasionally yellow colour. The roots come in a variety of shapes and sizes, some long and tapering, others small and almost globe-shaped. All species are widely used in cookery, raw and cooked. They are prepared as salads, soups and main dishes, and because of their sweet flavour can be used in drinks and cakes.
Carrot is a significant source of vitamin A, best absorbed from cooked carrots. Also present are vitamins B_1, B_2 and C (the last mainly in the centre of the root) as well as calcium, phosphorus, magnesium and iodine.

Celeriac

The white, thickened root crowns have a flavour resembling celery and can be made into salads, soups, hot and cold starters, main dishes and drinks. The green leaves can be used as a seasoning and garnish. Celeriac seeds are sometimes used as a spice. The cleaned tubers oxidize rapidly and must be put into cold water with lemon juice or vinegar added. Small, firm celeriacs are suitable for preparation in the raw form, while larger ones can be used for cooked dishes, sauces and soups.
Celeriac contains a small quantity of vitamin C (a high percentage is present in the leaves), vitamin A, vitamins B_1, B_2 and a large amount of calcium.

Horseradish

Horseradish has a distinct, slightly pungent taste. It is best used fresh to season salads, hot and cold starters, sauces, or to accompany boiled or fried meat, fish, eggs and cheese. It is often added to pickled vegetables. It is recommended to be served with fatty meals because of its alkaline properties. Horseradish is a significant source of vitamin C. It also contains potassium, sodium, calcium, manganese, iron, chlorine, phosphorus and sulphur. In addition it stimulates gastric activity.

Parsnip

The thickened, yellowish-white root has a sweetish taste resembling that of the carrot. It is used in salads, soups, casseroles, and wine can be made from it. It is rich in vitamin C and contains some vitamin A.

Radish

The thickened, tapering or globular root ranges in surface colour from the familiar red to yellow, white or even black. The raw white pulp, with a slightly pungent taste, is suitable for salads, starters or to garnish cold dishes. The juice mixed with honey is recommended as a cough medicine. Radish contains vitamin A and vitamins B_1, B_2 and C.

Salsify (Scorzonera)

The thickened, cylindrical root is eaten as a vegetable. The surface is dark brown to black, the inside white. The delicate taste is reminiscent of asparagus. Salads are made from raw salsify, and it is served cooked with butter, white sauces, au gratin, etc. It contains vitamin A, vitamin C, nitrogen, phosphorus and other trace minerals. It is easily digested and has a low chlorine content.

BRASSICA

Broccoli

Broccoli is a delicate vegetable resembling cauliflower. It does not form such large rosettes, but grows a few small, thickened inflorescences instead. Broccoli may be green (often called calabrese) but there are white and yellow varieties as well as the popular 'purple sprouting' spring variety. The mineral and vitamin content is similar to cauliflower. Broccoli also has a high quantity of vitamin E.

Brussels sprouts

This tasty vegetable is particularly valuable in winter. It tolerates frost and preserves its taste and biological properties at low temperatures. It may be served in salads as well as soups, side-dishes and main dishes. Brussels sprouts contain potassium, phosphorus, sulphur, a smaller quantity of iodine, etc. They have more vitamin C than the other brassicas. They also contain vitamin A and vitamins B_1, B_2 and K.

Cabbage, white or red

A popular vegetable, suitable for a variety of excellent salads, soups, main and side-dishes. Cabbage can be used fresh, fermented (sauerkraut) or pickled. Cabbage contains a high quantity of vitamin C, which is preserved in lactic fermentation. It has less vitamin A, vitamins B_1, B_2 and a small amount of vitamins E and K. Potassium, phosphorus, sulphur and calcium are the main minerals. Red cabbage is richer in vitamin A and vitamins of the B group than white cabbage. It is excellent as a colourful addition to salads or braised as an accompaniment to winter casseroles.

Cauliflower

A popular and valuable vegetable. The white, compact inflorescence is served cooked, with butter or white sauce. fried or au gratin.

Salads and starters can be made from small florets of raw cauliflower, pickled cauliflower and from cauliflower in brine. Cauliflower contains little cellulose, which makes it easy to digest. It contains quite a lot of vitamin C, less vitamin A and traces of vitamins B_1, D and K. It is rich in potassium, calcium and phosphorus.

Kale

Kale is grown for its crinkled leaves, hence the popular name 'curly kale'. Kale may be light or deep green or purplish. It has similar culinary uses to Savoy cabbage. It is also delicious dipped in flour, egg and breadcrumbs, and fried. Kale is richer in vitamins and minerals than Savoy cabbage.

Kohlrabi

There are many varieties of kohlrabi. The pale green type is most often found. But there are white and purple varieties as well. It is a significant source of vitamin C. It also contains vitamin A, vitamins B_1, B_2, and others. The leaves of young plants contain potassium, calcium, phosphorus, and more iron than spinach.

Small, early kohlrabi may be served raw as a cold starter or in salad. The chopped, fresh young leaves can be sprinkled over boiled potatoes or soups. Larger kohlrabi is prepared in the same way, but is more often cooked. It is served with melted butter or various sauces, stewed separately or with other vegetables or meat. Kohlrabi may also be stuffed.

Savoy cabbage

This valuable brassica with its attractive crinkly green leaves makes soups, side-dishes and main courses. It contains a high quantity of vitamin A, and less of vitamins B_1 and B_2, potassium, iron, sulphur, phosphorus and calcium.

PULSES

Beans

There is a wide selection of bean varieties: broad, runner and French being the most familiar. The shape and colour of the seeds differ — oval, kidney-shaped, roundish, white, yellow, brown, purplish, spotted or black. In runner and French beans it is unripe fresh pods which are eaten, whereas in broad beans the shelled young seeds are eaten, although very young broad beans may be eaten in the pod.

Fresh beans are rich in proteins and monosaccharides. They contain a large quantity of vitamins of the B group, but cooking and mainly preserving decrease the percentage.

A small amount of vitamin A is present, as well as vitamins C, K and E.

Peas

Peas are generally used for their mature (but never over-ripe) seeds. In some varieties such as mange tout or sugar peas the whole pods can be consumed. Raw peas have the most nutritional value and are delicious added to salads. Cooked peas make a good side-dish and can be used in soups.

Green peas are very rich in minerals, potassium, sodium, calcium, manganese, iron, phosphorus, chlorine and bromine. They contain a lot of sugar and vitamins of the B group, vitamin A, vitamins C and K.

SALAD VEGETABLES

Nearly all vegetables can be used cooked or raw in salads but the following are primarily used as salad vegetables.

Chicory

The blanched leaf heads are the edible parts of this salad vegetable. The white leaves have a delicately tart taste, the green ones are too bitter to be used. Chicory can be served in salads, cold and hot starters, and main dishes. Its quality decreases with exposure to daylight — it turns green and bitter — and should be stored wrapped in newspaper.

Chinese cabbage

This vegetable is usually served in salads, but it can be cooked like cabbage or spinach, added to soups, stuffed, served as a side-dish, etc. The thick ribs can be cooked like asparagus.

Dandelion

The young leaves of non-flowering plants are used in salads. The most tender and tasty leaves are produced by blanched dandelions, covered by rugs or straw during cultivation, but the leaves of wild plants can also be picked.

Besides vitamin A, dandelions also contain vitamin C (mainly in the unblanched green leaves), calcium, and some iron, potassium, etc.

Endive

Endive is usually eaten as a salad. The blanched leaves have a pleasant, slightly bitter taste. It is an important source of vitamins, mainly in autumn and winter. The content of minerals and vitamins is the same as in lettuce, but the percentage of vitamin C is higher.

Lettuce

Lettuce is one of the favourite salad vegetables. In addition to its refreshing taste, it is also a source of vitamins, mainly of vitamin A and vitamins B_1, B_2, B_6 and E. It has a smaller quantity of vitamin C (contained mainly in the outer leaves). Lettuce is rich in calcium and it contains iron, potassium and phosphorus. It is usually served in salads but it can be cooked in many tasty ways and makes a good soup.

SPINACH AND RELATED VEGETABLES

Spinach

Spinach leaves are usually served cooked, in soups, as side-dishes, soufflés, rolls, omelette fillings, etc. Spinach is a significant source of almost all the important vitamins (A, B, C, E, K) and minerals (iodine, iron, calcium, arsenic). Unfortunately it has a high content of oxalic acid which binds calcium and turns it into the insoluble calcium oxalate. Spinach must therefore be combined with calcium-rich foodstuffs, such as milk, cheese, cottage cheese and eggs. In order to preserve the minerals as much as possible, spinach should be cooked just in the liquid which clings to the leaves after washing. By immersing it in boiling water, up to 40 per cent of minerals are lost in the liquid.

Plum tomatoes are very useful for making sauces as well as being used in pizzas and other Italian dishes

In contrast here is a basket of salad tomatoes with a wedge of celeriac, a carrot, parsnip and onion

▶

A colourful selection of fresh vegetables makes an appetising sight

Nettle

The leaves of young wild nettles can be prepared as salads or soups, or cooked in the same way as spinach. They contain an exceptionally high quantity of iron. Also present are phosphorus, sodium, manganese, and other mineral components, as well as vitamin A and vitamin C.

Sorrel

The green, sometimes reddish leaves have a pleasant, slightly sour, refreshing taste. The young, tender spring leaves are of the best quality. They are served in salads, added to soups or cooked as spinach. Sorrel is very rich in vitamin A, contains vitamin C, and various other minerals. It should not be served to children or adults suffering from a kidney disease because of its high oxalic acid content.

Swiss chard

This vegetable is cultivated in two forms: the stalked chard has short, tender and thick white stalks, whereas the leaf variety has long, greenish stalks and larger leaves. The leaves are pale or dark green, sometimes with a reddish tinge. The cooked leaves are used in the same manner as spinach and are suitable for soups, side-dishes, omelettes and pastry fillings. The cooked stalks are served in the same manner as asparagus or celery, with hot sauces, au gratin, in soups, salads or cold starters. Swiss chard contains — mainly in the leaves — a large amount of vitamin A, vitamin C, iron, calcium, etc.

GOURDS

Cucumber

A popular, refreshing vegetable. It is usually served raw in salads and cold starters, sometimes mixed in cold drinks (such as Pimms). Hot cucumber dishes are less common but can be delicious. Fermented or pickled cucumbers seasoned by dill, tarragon, horseradish, maraschino cherry or vine leaves are very popular.

Cucumbers contain 95–98 per cent water and their nutritional value is consequently low. Some vitamin C is present mainly in the green skin, and there are traces of vitamins A and B. Pickled cucumbers are easier to digest than fresh ones.

Marrow

The fruits which exist in a variety of shapes can be prepared in many ways, from cold and hot starters, salads, soups, main dishes and side-dishes to desserts, compotes and drinks. For cooking both the fruits and the large, yellow bell-shaped flowers are used (for stuffing), as well as the oily seeds, and even the floury roots of some species. Pumpkin can be preserved in sugar, pickled in vinegar or wine, it can be made into alcoholic beverages by fermentation, or dried and ground into flour. The small, slender, cucumber-shaped forms called courgettes or zucchini are very popular and can be used in salads as well as a variety of cooked dishes. The flat, disc-like varieties called summer squashes or custard marrows are occasionally found in the shops and are easy for gardeners to grow.

MISCELLANEOUS VEGETABLES

Asparagus

Asparagus is a delicious, popular, if somewhat expensive vegetable. The young, unbranched shoots are eaten. Blanched asparagus is sometimes said to be tastier, but the green variety is more valuable biologically. Often served on its own with melted butter as a starter, it may also be served in salads, cold and hot starters, soups, and side-dishes. It is rich in minerals — potassium, phosphorus, iron, sulphur, sodium and silicon which is concentrated in the base. It contains vitamin C (mainly the heads), vitamin A, and vitamins B_1 and B_2. Its low calorific value makes it suitable for a slimming diet.

Aubergine

The most familiar are the elongated, purple, mauve or black fruits but aubergines may also be yellow, orange, brown or white and round or oval-shaped. The latter gave rise to the name 'eggplant'. They are used in vegetable stews and can be fried or baked with or without a stuffing. Aubergines are low in calories, having a water content of up to 92 per cent and therefore can make a useful contribution to a slimming diet, provided they are not fried as they tend to soak up large quantities of oil.

Cardoon

The blanched stalks of this edible thistle plant are very delicate and tasty. They are usually served cooked with various white sauces, or au gratin. Cardoon is rich in minerals, especially calcium, and in magnesium and potassium and is easy to digest.

Celery

The blanched, thickened leaf stalks of a whitish, yellow-green or green colour are served in salads, braised or used as flavouring for soups and casseroles. They are suitable for freezing. The underground parts of this variety are not used in cookery.

Celery contains minerals, particularly calcium, vitamin A, vitamin B_1, B_2 and a small quantity of vitamin C.

Fennel

Sometimes known as Florence fennel, the edible parts of this tasty vegetable is the swollen base of the leaf stalks which forms a sort of bulb. The flavour is mild and slightly aniseedy. Raw fennel is eaten as a salad. The bulbs can be stuffed with various fillings and stewed. The chopped young leaves, similar in shape to dill leaves, are used to garnish salads and hot dishes. Fennel contains a high quantity of vitamin C, iron and magnesium.

Globe artichoke

The edible parts of this perennial plant are the thickened flower receptacles with large bracts. They can be cooked, stuffed, baked, preserved in oil or pickled. They are an important vegetable from the point of nutrition, containing vitamin A, vitamins of the B group, some vitamin C, iron, and substances preventing the settling of cholesterol in the arteries. Traditionally, artichokes have been regarded as an aphrodisiac.

Hop

In some countries the young root shoots of the hop vine grown in fields are used in a similar way to asparagus. The most delicate and tender raw shoots are served in salads. Cooked hop shoots are eaten as a hot starter or side-dish. They contain calcium, sodium, phosphorus and other minerals, vitamin A, vitamins B_1, B_2 and a small quantity of vitamin C.

Peppers

Like tomatoes, peppers are popular throughout the world. They are cultivated in many varieties, colours, sizes and tastes. The taste ranges from sweet to slightly pungent and very hot. The sweet, mild varieties are eaten in salads, starters, soups, sauces, marinades and main dishes; the hot and spicy ones are sparingly used to season mixed salads, sauces, stews, etc. All varieties can be pickled or preserved in oil, in brine, or dried.

Unripe, green peppers are very rich in vitamin C and contain some vitamin A. The percentage of vitamin A increases up to ten times in ripe fruits.

Herbs can be successfully grown in the garden or, as here, in pots which can be placed on the window ledge of the kitchen

These thick slices of celeriac should be sprinkled with lemon juice as soon as they are cut to prevent discoloration

This selection of vegetables would make a very good vegetable soup

Rhubarb

This is one of the few species of vegetables prepared only as a sweet dish, hence it is generally thought of as a fruit. The thickened stalks, green, pink or red, are the only parts used and the large leaves are actually poisonous. The red stalks have a finer flavour, but they are thinner than the green ones. Rhubarb can be stewed, bottled, made into jams, pastry fillings and drinks. It is rich in vitamins A and C, potassium, phosphorus and magnesium. Malic and oxalic acids provide it with a refreshing taste but too much oxalic acid interferes with the absorption of calcium by the body.

Sweetcorn

The mature but unripe cobs of the garden maize are used either whole, or just the kernels can be removed. The cobs are usually served raw, marinated or boiled. Corn can be preserved in brine or pickled. It contains relatively little vitamin A, vitamin B_2, potassium, sodium and phosphorus, but it is rich in easily digestible proteins and sugars.

Tomato

The tomato is actually a fruit though it is universally regarded as a vegetable. It comes in many varieties — from tiny cherry tomatoes, hardly as big as a thumb nail, to large tomatoes measuring over 10 cm/4 in in diameter. The fruits are predominantly red, in various shades, but there are varieties with white, yellow or purplish fruits.

Tomatoes are used in cookery in many ways. They are served in salads, starters, soups, main dishes, sauces, desserts, drinks, etc. They are rich in vitamin A, contain vitamins B_1, C, potassium, sodium, calcium, iron, copper, etc. The alkaloid solanine is found in unripe, green tomatoes; it must not be consumed in large quantities. It is present mostly in the skin and can be easily removed by peeling green fruits.

HERBS

Basil

Fresh or dried leaves of this aromatic plant are used to season vegetable salads, soups, game, fish, pizza, etc. The flavour goes particularly well with tomato and is used a great deal in Italian cooking. It is one of the seasonings in smoked products. Basil is said to improve the appetite and gastric function, and prevent flatulence.

Bay leaves

The dried leaves of the bay tree are used to flavour many dishes, including soups, stews and sauces. A bay leaf is an essential ingredient for a bouquet garni. Fresh bay leaves can be used as a garnish — for example a pâté or terrine will always look well with a couple of small bay leaves on top.

Chervil

The slightly pungent, sweetish chervil leaves (similar to parsley) are suitable for salads, egg dishes, soups and fish. Roast or grilled meat and poultry can be seasoned with dried chervil. It is a good flavouring for dishes made of cottage cheese, including sweet ones.

Dill

A highly popular herb with a mild aniseed flavour. Young leaves are used to flavour salads, spreads, soups, sauces, etc. Older plants, after flowering, are used for pickling vegetables. Salads and grilled meats can be seasoned with finely ground dill seeds. Dill can be stored in the dried form or preserved in salt and vinegar. It contains a large quantity of vitamin C, stimulates the appetite and it is reputed to have calming effects.

Marjoram

Sweet marjoram is a plant native to the Mediterranean whose leaves can be used fresh or dried. It is a herb frequently used in French, Italian and Greek cooking with lamb, white meat, sauces and tomato dishes.

Oregano

This form of wild marjoram has a heady scent and flavour. The dried form is most famous for its use in pizzas and other Italian dishes.

Parsley

The familiar green leaves and sometimes the dried seeds are used to season soups, salads, cold and hot dishes. Parsley makes an excellent garnish for various dishes.

The roots are also eaten in some countries and are rich in vitamin A. The leaves are a good source of vitamin C. An abundance of minerals is found in the whole plant — iron, sulphur, magnesium, manganese, etc.

Peppermint

Peppermint is a perennial plant, a multiple hybrid of several wild mint species. Both the fresh, young leaves and dried leaves are used as a seasoning. Peppermint goes well with many soups, salads, sauces, meat, fish, cheese, and it aromatizes drinks. A tasty herb tea can be prepared from peppermint. The plant contains a high percentage of vitamin A.

Tarragon

This plant can be used either fresh or dried, though the former is, of course, the best alternative wherever possible. It is an aromatic plant which is ideal for egg and cream dishes, with salad, chicken or ham. It can also be used to make tarragon vinegar.

Cutting root vegetables

Special equipment for cutting vegetables

Cutting radishes for garnish

Preparing horseradish (Horse-radish and beetroot relish, Horseradish and apple relish, Horseradish cream)

Shredding cabbage

Cleaning, slicing and shaping of vegetables

CLEANING

Vegetables supply the human body with vital minerals and vitamins. To prevent unnecessary losses and to preserve the typical taste and look of vegetables, certain rules have to be observed during cleaning:

– Clean vegetables just before preparation.

– Clean vegetables in one piece (before separating them into parts).

– Always wash vegetables in cold running water.

– Never soak vegetables in water; this causes the minerals to dissolve.

– Use sharp knives and peelers.

– Wash salad vegetables in cold running water, drain them in a sieve, and dry in a clean tea-towel if necessary.

– A knife can be used to cut salad vegetables, but it is preferable to tear lettuce up into small pieces.

– Scrub root vegetables with a brush in cold running water and peel them with a sharp knife or peeler (young, fresh vegetables can just be thoroughly scrubbed and washed).

– Before peeling tomatoes or peppers, plunge them into boiling water for a few seconds. Alternatively, peppers can be quickly roasted on a hotplate or grilled.

– Cut off the tips of artichoke leaves and the top and bottom of the artichoke, brush the cut surfaces with lemon juice, or apply lemon slices and fasten them with string.

– Peel salsify from the top downwards, taking care not to break it to prevent the loss of juice; put the cleaned salsify into water with vinegar or lemon, or into sour milk, to stop it turning black.

– Clean asparagus spears with a sharp peeler or knife from the top downwards; tie up spears of the same size in a bundle before cooking for easier handling.

– Remove the withered leaves and roots of leeks, cut them lengthways and wash thoroughly. This applies mainly to older large leeks which may have been stored in sand.

SLICING AND SHAPING

Appropriate care must be taken in slicing and shaping vegetables. To ensure even cooking, the cut pieces must be of the same size.

Root vegetables and kohlrabi for salads and soups are cut into thin strips or diced, or finely grated. If served as a side-dish, they are cut into dice, chips or triangles. Young, fresh carrots can be served whole. Vegetables for soup stock should be sliced or grated. Vegetable balls or olives can be scooped out with special utensils. Various shapes can be cut out from carrot or kohlrabi, or other vegetables, with pastry cutters, to garnish a variety of dishes.

Cabbage is quartered, the stalk removed and the leaves either finely shredded with a knife or grated. For some salads and hot dishes, cabbage is cut into squares.

PREPARATION OF VEGETABLES FOR STUFFING

Celeriac

Smaller roots of celeriac should be used for stuffing. Boil in salted water until tender (about 45 minutes). Allow to cool slightly, then cut the top off and scoop out the inside.

Tomatoes

A lid is sliced off from firm equal-sized tomatoes and the inside is scooped out. Replace the lid after stuffing the tomatoes. For cold starters, marinate tomatoes in oil, vinegar and salt for 5–10 minutes.

Cucumbers, pumpkins, aubergine

For hot dishes, cut the vegetables lengthways and scoop out the pulp with a spoon. Stuff both halves, press together and tie with thread. Alternatively arrange the cut halves in an ovenproof dish and pile the stuffing into them. The vegetables can additionally be wrapped in aluminium foil. Young cucumbers and aubergine do not have to be peeled. Wash thoroughly and cut off the stalks. Pumpkin is tough-skinned and must be peeled.

For cold dishes, cucumbers are sliced into rounds or obliquely into 5-cm/2-in segments, and most of the pulp is scooped out. Tender greenhouse cucumbers do not need peeling. Cucumbers can be marinated in salt, oil and vinegar for 5–10 minutes, like tomatoes.

Leafy vegetables

Select large leaves of cabbage, spinach, chard etc. and blanch them in lightly salted boiling water for about 2 minutes. Drain them and slightly crush the thick ribs with a meat beater, if necessary.

Savoy cabbage

The whole head is boiled in salted water until tender (15–20 minutes) and drained in a sieve. Place the cabbage on a wooden board, spread the leaves and put the filling between them. Re-form the head into its original shape and tie up with string or wrap in foil. Spring cabbage can be prepared in the same way.

Cauliflower

Boil a firm, compact head of cauliflower in salted water until tender (15–20 minutes) and drain. Put it into a bowl or sieve as large as the cauliflower, turn it upside down and scoop the stalk out with a metal spoon. Smaller heads of late cabbage may be prepared for stuffing in the same way.

Peppers

For cold dishes, cut the peppers in half lengthways and remove the seeds and pith. Marinate in oil, vinegar and salt for 10–15 minutes. For hot dishes, cut off a lid at the stalk end and scoop out the seeds and pith. Stuff the peppers and replace the cut-off tops.

Onion

Boil even-sized onions in salted water until tender (50–60 minutes, depending on size), cut off the tops and scoop out the pulp. Stuff the onions and replace the lids.

Radishes

Make three deep, crossways notches on the root end of big radishes and put them into cold salted water. After a while the radishes will open and they can be stuffed with a variety of cold mousses by means of a piping bag.

Stuffing cauliflower

◄

Cooking artichokes

Stuffing cucumbers

Peeling asparagus

Fennel

The thickened stalks of this plant should be separated and used as receptacles for the stuffing. For cold fillings, marinate the fennel in oil, vinegar, salt, adding pepper and Worcestershire or soy sauce if desired, for 10–15 minutes. If using hot do not marinate fennel before cooking, just separate the stalks and sprinkle with salt.

Cooking methods

Blanching

Plunge the vegetables into a large pan filled with boiling salted water for 1 to 3 minutes. This destroys any undesirable bitter taste and speeds up cooking in the case of some stuffed vegetables. Take care that leaf vegetables do not soften too much in the process. Tomatoes and peppers which have been blanched for a few seconds and then plunged into cold water are easy to peel.

Boiling

Put the vegetables into boiling salted water and rapidly bring the water back to the boil. Vegetables should be boiled in a small quantity of water to preserve nutrients. Boil the vegetables uncovered to preserve their colour. Always try to choose even-sized vegetables when cooking them whole, or some will be overcooked and others underdone. The same rule applies to vegetables cut into pieces. When cooked drain the vegetables immediately, preserving the stock for soups or sauces if desired.

Vegetables can also be cooked in meat stock, wine, milk, etc. Never overcook vegetables — they lose not only their nutritional value, but also their taste and colour. Never cook vegetables in cracked enamelled pots or iron vessels.

Steaming

Loss of flavour, colour, vitamins and minerals is minimized by steaming. Either a steamer is used (a double vessel consisting of a pan with a sieve-like bottom and a larger pan in which the water is boiled), or a sieve or a perforated plate is placed in a pan with a little water.

Cooking in a bain-marie

The bain-marie or water bath consists of a bowl placed in a saucepan half filled with boiling water. This method of cooking is used for vegetable moulds and soufflés. The food is placed in a greased dish (tin mould, china or glass bowl), covered, and put in the pan with water, which is slowly heated. The water must not boil, or the texture of the food would be spoilt. It is kept just below boiling point. Alternatively the bain-marie may be placed in a moderate or cool oven. To prevent the formation of a hard crust, cover the dish with greased paper or foil.

Barbecuing

This method is not widely used for cooking vegetables, but they do acquire a delicious flavour. Thread the vegetables onto a spit or skewers, between slices of meat, fish, salami or bacon, or put pieces of vegetables dipped in oil (seasoned as desired) on the rack and baste with oil during cooking.

Baking in foil

Aluminium foil is used mainly for stuffed vegetables or for vegetable mixtures containing meat or fish. The advantage of this method is that all the flavour is preserved. The vegetables must be tightly sealed in the foil so that no air can get in.

*Stuffed peppers
in roasting bag*

*Aubergine in roasting
bag*

▶

*Preparing vegetables
for frying*

Braising

Braising is cooking in a covered vessel with the minimum of water over a low heat. Vegetables cut into even-sized pieces are lightly fried in fat. A little water, stock or milk is added and cooking completed in a covered pan. Do not add extra liquid when stewing vegetables with a high water content, such as tomato, pumpkin or cucumber. The heat releases their juice which is sufficient for the cooking. Braising must be done at a low temperature to avoid burning. Do not remove the lid too often as this causes valuable juices to escape and prolongs the cooking time. The vegetables must be cut into equal pieces to ensure even cooking.

Choose the frying fat according to the type of vegetable. Delicate vegetables, such as young carrots, peas or mushrooms are best fried in butter, while more robust vegetables, such as cabbage or leeks, may be fried in dripping or bacon fat.

Roasting, baking and shallow frying

Vegetables are put in a flameproof dish with a little fat and put into a hot oven. Only a limited number of vegetables are suitable for roasting, i.e. potatoes and parsnips. Some vegetables may be stuffed and baked (i.e. aubergines, courgettes, peppers).

Vegetables can also be shallow-fried in an open pan in a little fat. It is preferable to blanch most vegetables in salted water before roasting or baking but not shallow-frying.

Cooking in roasting bags

No loss of flavour occurs when vegetables are cooked by this method, no fat is used, and there is less washing up after the meal. Cleaned and seasoned vegetables, usually stuffed or mixed with meat, poultry, fish, etc., are placed in the bag. This is sealed with the supplied fastening and the bag is pricked in a few places. The dish is then cooked at the temperature recommended on the package. The dish can be prepared in advance, stored in the freezer and put straight into the oven. In that case the cooking time must be lengthened accordingly.

Baking au gratin

The vegetables are first boiled or braised. They are then seasoned and placed in a greased ovenproof dish. A sauce is poured over, the dish dotted with butter and quickly baked under a grill or in a very hot oven until golden and bubbling. To produce a crisp crust sprinkle the dish with breadcrumbs just before baking. Whole beaten eggs or egg yolks mixed with grated cheese can be used instead of a sauce or eggs and milk, cream or yogurt can be used. Alternatively the dish can be sprinkled with grated cheese such as Parmesan or Emmental.

Deep frying

Almost all kinds of vegetables are suitable for frying. The harder vegetables, such as cauliflower, carrots and Savoy cabbage, should be blanched first. Celeriac and peppers are sprinkled with salt and left to become more tender. Some vegetables are dipped in the batter raw (pumpkin, parsley leaves, etc.).

Vegetables are either dipped in flour, beaten egg and fine dry breadcrumbs, or in a batter made from milk, flour, eggs, a little oil and salt. White wine or pale ale can be used instead of milk, and finely chopped ham, salami or almonds can be added.

Oil or pure vegetable fat should be used for frying, as they do not burn easily. Fill the deep-frier no more than two-thirds full of fat and fry small quantities of vegetable at a time. Take care not to overheat the oil. The fried vegetables should be drained thoroughly on absorbent kitchen paper to soak up excess fat.

Stir-frying

This method of quick frying is usually associated with Chinese cooking. It is traditionally done in a wok — a deep, steep-sided frying pan with a large surface area. The vegetables to be used should be cut into fine, evenly sized pieces and are then tossed into the small amount of fat which has been pre-heated in the wok. Stir-frying is a very quick way of cooking vegetables so the nutritional contents are not lost.

Cooking in a microwave oven

Most vegetables cook very well in a microwave and the results are often better than by employing conventional cooking methods. Vegetables can be put into a roasting bag or dish with only a small amount of liquid or a knob of butter. The full flavour of the fresh vegetables is retained and the vegetables will often cook in a fraction of the time taken normally e.g. in baking potatoes.

▲ *Preparing celeriac with salami*
  for frying
◄ *Barbecueing vegetables*
  in the open air

Cooking in aluminium-foil bowls

Steaming and frying vegetables

Cold starters

Asparagus with piquant dressing

1 (340-g/12-oz) can asparagus spears
25 g/1 oz pickled onions
25 g/1 oz gherkins
2 anchovies, mashed
4 tablespoons oil
1–2 tablespoons lemon juice
salt and freshly ground black pepper
1 tablespoon finely chopped parsley

Arrange the asparagus in a glass dish. Finely chop the onions and gherkins and mix with the anchovies. Mix the oil with the lemon juice to taste and season with salt and pepper, remembering that the anchovies are fairly salty. Add the dressing to the onion mixture and stir in the parsley. Finally pour the dressing over the asparagus. Chill well before serving.

French beans with dill

350 g/12 oz French beans
For the marinade:
1 large onion, finely chopped
4 tablespoons oil
1–2 tablespoons vinegar
2 tablespoons chopped dill
salt and freshly ground black pepper

String the beans and cook in boiling salted water for 5–10 minutes until just tender. Drain. Mix together the ingredients for the marinade and pour over the beans. Marinate for 2 hours, turning the beans occasionally.

Peppers with beef salad

2 red or green peppers
salt
100 g/4 oz cold roast beef, cut into strips
50 g/2 oz gherkins, chopped
1 hard-boiled egg, chopped
1 tablespoon oil
2 teaspoons mild prepared mustard
2 tomatoes, sliced
1 tablespoon chopped parsley

Halve, core, wash and drain the peppers and sprinkle the insides with salt. Mix together the beef, gherkins and hard-boiled egg. Whisk together the oil and mustard and stir into the beef mixture. Pile this into the halved peppers and garnish with tomato slices and chopped parsley.

Vegetable-stuffed trout
(Illustrated on page 38)

1 (350-g/12-oz) trout
50 g/2 oz white bread, with crusts removed
2 tablespoons double cream
1 egg, lightly beaten
salt and white pepper
pinch ground mace
1 small carrot, diced
25 g/1 oz frozen peas
25 g/1 oz frozen sweetcorn
1½ teaspoons powdered gelatine
4 tablespoons white wine
Garnish:
    cucumber balls, lemon slices, leek or spring onion, peeled cooked prawns, radishes, pickled corn cobs

Bone and fillet the trout and arrange the fillets skin side down on foil. Dice the bread, moisten it with cream and add the eggs, seasoning to taste and mace. Blanch the carrot, peas and sweetcorn in boiling water for 2 minutes, then drain and cool. Dissolve the gelatine in 2 tablespoons hot, but not boiling, water and add to the wine. Fold the blanched vegetables into the stuffing and quickly add the wine mixture. Spread the stuffing over the trout fillets and roll up the foil, pressing the fillets together. Seal the edges of the foil to make a watertight parcel and put the roll into hot water and simmer gently for 20–25 minutes, being careful not to let the water boil. Cool, remove the foil and slice the fish. Garnish with a selection of the suggested ingredients.

Cheese cornets with vegetables

(Illustrated on page 38)

50 g/2 oz butter
100 g/4 oz cream cheese
salt
1 teaspoon chopped chives
8 slices Edam cheese
Garnish:
   tomato wedges, olives, radish slices, celery sticks, miniature corn cobs, parsley sprigs

Cream the butter with the cream cheese. Season to taste with salt and add the chives. Pile the mixture into a piping bag fitted with a star nozzle. Roll the Edam cheese into cornet shapes and pipe the cream cheese mixture into them. Arrange on a plate and garnish with a selection of the suggested vegetables.

Peppers with cheese salad

(Illustrated on page 39)

2 medium green peppers
50 g/2 oz cooked ham
75 g/3 oz Edam cheese
1 tomato, peeled and deseeded
50 g/2 oz pickled silverskin onions
50 g/2 oz cream cheese
1 tablespoon double cream
salt and freshly ground black pepper
Garnish:
   chives, pepper rings, tomato wedges, button mushrooms, parsley sprigs

Halve the peppers and remove the seeds. Cut the ham, cheese and tomato into strips, add the onions and mix with the cream cheese and cream. Season to taste with salt and pepper. Stuff the pepper shells with the cheese mixture and garnish with the suggested vegetables.

Variation:
Peppers with vegetable cheese salad

Omit the Edam cheese, onions and ham and add 4 radishes, 1 small carrot and 1 small dessert apple, all finely grated, to the cream cheese mixture.

Artichokes with garlic dressing

(Illustrated on page 39)

3 tablespoons oil
1 tablespoon lemon juice
salt and freshly ground white pepper
50 g/2 oz finely chopped onion
2 cloves garlic, crushed
1 tablespoon finely chopped chives
1 (312-g/11-oz can) artichoke bottoms
tomato slices to garnish

Whisk together the oil and lemon juice and season to taste with salt and pepper. Add the onion, garlic and chives and mix well. Arrange the artichokes on a serving dish and pour over a little of the dressing. Garnish with tomato and hand the rest of the dressing separately.

Tomato cream with cucumber

100 g/4 oz cream cheese
1 tablespoon concentrated tomato purée
salt
2 tomatoes, peeled, deseeded and chopped
100 ml/4 fl oz double cream
cucumber slices to garnish

Mix the cream cheese with the tomato purée and season to taste with salt. Add the tomatoes and cream and turn the mixture into individual glass dishes. Garnish each dish with a fan-shaped slice of cucumber.

Vegetable-stuffed trout

Cheese cornets with vegetables

Peppers with cheese salad

Artichokes with garlic dressing

Peppers with vegetable stuffing

2 red or green peppers
1 small onion
1 medium carrot
50 g/2 oz celeriac
1 tomato
1 (5-cm/2-in) piece cucumber
2 tablespoons oil
1 tablespoon lemon juice
2 teaspoons concentrated tomato purée
salt
1 tablespoon chopped dill or parsley

Halve and deseed the peppers. Dice the onion, finely grate the carrot and celeriac and slice the tomato and cucumber. Arrange the vegetables in a dish. Whisk together the oil, lemon juice and tomato purée. Season to taste with salt and stir in the dill or parsley. Pour the dressing over the vegetables and toss gently. Pile the mixture into the peppers.

Cheese cornets with yogurt and vegetable stuffing

4 slices Edam cheese (total weight 100 g/4 oz)
3 tablespoons double cream
3 tablespoons natural yogurt
salt and freshly ground white pepper

2 teaspoons finely chopped chives
½ green pepper, diced
1 tomato, peeled, deseeded and diced
4 radishes to garnish

Form the slices of Edam into cornets. Lightly whip the cream and stir in the yogurt. Season to taste with salt and pepper. Add the chopped chives and fold in the pepper and tomato. Fill the cheese cornets with this mixture. Garnish each cornet with a decoratively shaped radish (see page 23).

Tomatoes stuffed with cauliflower

4 large tomatoes
100 g/4 oz cauliflower, broken into small florets
50 g/2 oz cream cheese
2 tablespoons mayonnaise
50 g/2 oz cocktail onions, finely chopped
1 teaspoon fresh chopped tarragon or ½ teaspoon dried tarragon
salt and freshly ground white pepper

Blanch the tomatoes in boiling water for a few seconds, then cool and peel. Cut off the top to make a lid and scoop out the seeds. Blanch the cauliflower in boiling water for 2 minutes, drain and cool. Mix the cream cheese with the mayonnaise and add the chopped onions and tarragon. Season to taste with salt and pepper. Carefully

fold in the cauliflower and use the mixture to fill the tomatoes.

Tomatoes with sardine stuffing

4 medium tomatoes
salt
50 g/2 oz butter
75 g/3 oz canned sardines, mashed
20 cocktail onions
1 hard-boiled egg, finely chopped
1–2 teaspoons lemon juice
chopped chives to garnish

Blanch and peel the tomatoes. Cut off the tops, scoop out the seeds and sprinkle the shells with salt. Cream the butter and mix in the sardines, onions and egg. Season to taste with lemon juice and pile the mixture into the tomato shells. Garnish with chopped chives.

Fruit-filled tomatoes

4 large tomatoes
salt
50 g/2 oz butter
75 g/3 oz cream cheese
2 tablespoons double cream
1 dessert apple, peeled and grated
Garnish:
    4 segments canned mandarin orange or fresh satsuma
    4 walnut halves
    4 sprigs parsley

Blanch and peel the tomatoes, slice off the tops and scoop out the seeds. Sprinkle the shells lightly with salt. Cream together the butter and cream cheese. Stir in the double cream and apple. Pile the mixture into the tomato shells and top with a segment of mandarin orange, a walnut half and a sprig of parsley.

Tomatoes with celery and almond filling

4 large tomatoes
2 sticks celery
1 small dessert apple
salt
50 g/2 oz cream cheese
2 tablespoons mayonnaise
8 blanched almonds
4 sprigs parsley

Blanch and peel the tomatoes. Cut off the top third and scoop out the seeds. Cut the celery and apple into thin strips and salt to taste. Mix the cream cheese with the mayonnaise and carefully fold in the apple and celery. Fill the tomatoes with the celery salad and garnish with almonds and a sprig of parsley.

Vegetable cheese

225 g/8 oz cottage or curd cheese
1 medium carrot, finely grated
50 g/2 oz celeriac, finely grated

25 g/1 oz horseradish or radish, finely grated
1 tomato, peeled, deseeded and chopped
salt
1–2 teaspoons lemon juice
1 tablespoon finely chopped chives
100 ml/4 fl oz double cream

Lightly mix the cheese with the carrot, celeriac, horseradish or radish and tomato. Add salt and lemon juice to taste and fold in the chopped chives. Stir in the cream. The mixture can be served with slices of crisp toast and is excellent as a stuffing for vegetables, or ham or cheese cornets.

Eggs with tomato cream

4 hard-boiled eggs
75 g/3 oz cream cheese
50 g/2 oz butter
1 tablespoon concentrated tomato purée
2 tablespoons double cream
salt
Garnish:
    tomato wedges
    spring onions, chopped

Slice the hard-boiled eggs lengthways and scoop out the yoke. Mash the yolk and mix with the cream cheese, butter and tomato purée. Stir in the cream and season to taste with salt. Use the mixture to fill the halved egg whites, piping through a star nozzle, if desired.

Garnish with the tomato wedges and spring onions.

Tomatoes with carrot salad

4 tomatoes, peeled
50 g/2 oz cream cheese
3 tablespoons double cream
2 medium carrots, diced
1 dessert apple, peeled and diced
salt
4 walnuts to garnish

Cut the tops off the tomatoes and scoop out the seeds. Beat the cream cheese with the double cream and fold in the carrot and apple. Add salt to taste. Fill the tomato shells and garnish with walnuts.

Peppers with liver pâté

2 green peppers
50 g/2 oz butter
75 g/3 oz smooth liver pâté
3 tablespoons double cream
salt
4 black olives
tomato wedges

Halve and deseed the peppers. Cream the butter with the liver pâté and fold in the cream. Season to taste with salt. Divide the mixture between the pepper halves and top with a black olive and wedges of tomato.

Tomato aspic with vegetables

Ham cornets
with tomato aspic

(Illustrated at bottom left)

Set half quantity of the basic recipe in four individual moulds and turn out into serving plates. Form 4 (25-g/1-oz) slices of cooked ham into cornets around the jellies. Garnish with piquant vegetables such as cocktail onions, gherkins, chillies etc.

Tomato aspic
(basic recipe)

(Illustrated on page 43)

450 g/1 lb tomatoes
200 ml/7 fl oz stock (vegetable or
    chicken)
15 g/$\frac{1}{2}$ oz gelatine
100 ml/4 fl oz double cream
juice of $\frac{1}{2}$ lemon
salt and freshly ground black pepper

Blanch the tomatoes, cool and peel. Roughly chop the flesh, then liquidize in a blender or food processor. Sieve the purée to remove the seeds. Heat the stock almost to boiling point, then remove from the heat, allow to cool for a minute and sprinkle over the gelatine. Stir until the gelatine has completely dissolved. Allow to cool until the mixture becomes syrupy. Fold in the puréed tomatoes, double cream and lemon juice and season to

Ham cornets with tomato aspic

taste. Pour into wetted moulds and chill in the refrigerator until set. Turn out of the moulds and garnish with vegetables of your choice, for example olives, cucumber, tomato wedges, miniature corn cobs, parsley sprigs.

Variations:

Tomato aspic with vegetables

(Illustrated on page 42)

Fold in 50 g/2 oz cooked sweetcorn, 50 g/2 oz cooked peas and 25 g/1 oz cocktail onions to the basic tomato aspic when the mixture is beginning to thicken. Pour into a wetted mould and chill until firm. Serve cut into wedges, garnished with vegetables of your choice.

Stuffed tomatoes with ham

(Illustrated at top right)

4 medium tomatoes
25 g/1 oz butter
25 g/1 oz cream cheese
25 g/1 oz Danish blue cheese
1 tablespoon double cream
salt
4 cocktail onions to garnish

Blanch and peel the tomatoes, then cut off the lids and scoop out the seeds. Cream the butter and cream cheese. Mash the blue cheese and

Tomato aspic

add to the cream cheese mixture. Stir in the cream and season to taste with salt. Fill the tomatoes with the mixture and top with a cornet made from a slice of ham. Garnish with cocktail onions.

Tomatoes with chive and ham stuffing

4 tomatoes
150 g/5 oz cream cheese
3 tablespoons double cream
salt
50 g/2 oz cooked ham, chopped
1 tablespoon chopped chives

Blanch and peel the tomatoes. Cut off the lids and scoop out the seeds. Mix the cream cheese with the double cream, and season to taste with salt. Fold in the chopped ham and the chives. Stuff the tomatoes with the cheese mixture and replace the lids.

Stuffed cucumbers

75 g/3 oz boiled potatoes
1 medium carrot, grated
50 g/2 oz cooked beetroot, diced
1 small onion, diced
2 tablespoons oil
1–2 teaspoons vinegar
salt and freshly ground black pepper
1 cucumber
100 ml/4 fl oz soured cream
parsley sprigs to garnish

Dice the potatoes and place in a bowl with the carrot, beetroot and onion. Whisk together the oil and vinegar and season to taste with salt and freshly ground black pepper. Pour the dressing over the salad and toss gently. Cut the cucumber into diagonal slices about 1 cm/$\frac{1}{2}$ in thick and pile the salad on top of them. Top with soured cream and garnish with a sprig of parsley.

Mixed vegetable cocktail

$\frac{1}{2}$ small lettuce, shredded
100 g/4 oz red or green peppers, deseeded
100 g/4 oz tomatoes, blanched and peeled
100 g/4 oz cucumber
2 tablespoons mayonnaise
2 tablespoons yogurt
2 tablespoons double cream
1 tablespoon finely chopped chives
salt
4 wedges lemon to garnish

Line four cocktail glasses or individual glass dishes with shredded lettuce. Cut the peppers, tomatoes and cucumber into strips and pile into the glasses. Mix together the mayonnaise, yogurt and cream. Fold in the chopped chives and salt to taste. Pour the dressing over the vegetables and divide the salad between the four dishes. Garnish each glass with a wedge of lemon. Serve with crusty French bread or cheese straws.

Cucumber mould

450 g/1 lb cucumber
75 g/3 oz cocktail onions, finely chopped
salt and freshly ground black pepper
juice of $\frac{1}{2}$ lemon
15 g/$\frac{1}{2}$ oz gelatine
200 ml/7 fl oz vegetable or chicken stock
100 ml/4 fl oz soured cream
1 tablespoon finely chopped chives

Peel and coarsely grate the cucumber. Add the onions, salt, pepper and lemon juice. Dissolve the gelatine in 3 tablespoons hot, but not boiling, water and add to the stock, stirring well. When the liquid becomes syrupy pour over the cucumber mixture and stir well. Pour into a wetted mould and chill in the refrigerator until set. Turn out onto a serving dish and top with soured cream and chopped chives.

Vegetable salad with beef

75 g/3 oz carrots
75 g/3 oz celeriac
1 tablespoon oil
4 tablespoons tomato ketchup
salt and freshly ground black pepper
1–2 teaspoons vinegar
75 g/3 oz French beans, cut into 2.5-cm/1-in pieces
225 g/8 oz cold roast beef
50 g/2 oz cocktail onions

Cut the carrots and celeriac into thin strips. Heat the oil in a frying pan, then fry the carrot and celeriac over a medium to high heat, stirring all the time, until just beginning to soften. Remove from the heat and add the ketchup. Season with salt, pepper and vinegar. Cook over a low heat for a further 1–2 minutes. Allow the mixture to cool. Cook the beans in boiling water for a few minutes until just beginning to soften. Drain and cool. Cut the beef into strips and add to the tomato mixture. Stir in the beans and cocktail onions, toss and chill.

Pumpkin cocktail with dill

(Illustrated on page 46)

450 g/1 lb pumpkin or marrow
dash vinegar
2 tablespoons lemon juice
salt
100 ml/4 fl oz natural yogurt
1 tablespoon chopped fresh dill or
  mint
Garnish:
  lemon slices
  dill or mint sprigs

Peel the pumpkin or marrow, discard the seeds and dice the flesh. Blanch for 3–4 minutes in boiling salted water to which a dash of vinegar has been added. Drain, sprinkle with lemon juice and salt, cool and chill for a few hours. Mix together the yogurt and dill or mint and season with salt. Place the pumpkin or marrow in glasses and pour over the dressing. Garnish with slices of lemon and a sprig of dill or mint.

Stuffed cucumber with garlic sausage

(Illustrated on page 46)

225 g/8 oz cucumber
salt
50 g/2 oz butter
75 g/3 oz cream cheese
50 g/2 oz garlic sausage, sliced

Peel the cucumber and cut into four equal-sized pieces. Scoop out some of the pulp and salt the insides. Cream the butter with the cream cheese and use this mixture to fill the cucumbers, piping through a star nozzle if desired. Garnish with slices of garlic sausage.

Tomatoes with olives

(Illustrated on page 47)

2 large plum tomatoes, peeled
½ cucumber, peeled
40 g/1½ oz butter
50 g/2 oz cream cheese
3 tablespoons double cream
salt
paprika
4 black olives to garnish

Cut the rounded ends off the tomatoes and reserve. Cut the remaining pieces in half to make two thick slices. Cut four thick slices diagonally from the cucumber. Cream the butter with the cream cheese and add the double cream. Season to taste with salt and paprika. Place the tomato slices on a serving dish and use a little of the cheese mixture to sandwich each one together with a cucumber slice. Top with the rest of the cheese mixture, piping through a star nozzle if desired. Garnish with olives and the reserved slices of tomato.

Tomatoes with ham spread and cucumber

4 medium tomatoes
100 g/4 oz cooked ham
50 g/2 oz butter
2 tablespoons double cream
salt and freshly ground white pepper
Garnish:
  chopped chives
  cucumber

Blanch and peel the tomatoes. Cut off the tops and scoop out the seeds. Mince the ham finely. Cream the butter and work in the ham, moistening the mixture with double cream. Season to taste with salt and pepper. Use the mixture to stuff the tomatoes, piping through a star nozzle, if desired. Garnish with chopped chives and slices or balls of cucumber. The pale green part of a leek may be used as an alternative to chives.

Pumpkin cocktail with dill

Stuffed cucumber with garlic sausage
Tomatoes with ham spread
and cucumber
Kohlrabi stuffed with vegetable salad

Open sandwiches with radish, kohl-rabi, tomatoes and olive, garlic butter
Crispbread with herb spread

Tomatoes with olives
Tomatoes with ham spread and walnuts
Cucumber with cream cheese and radish
Kohlrabi stuffed with savoury salad

Variation:
Tomatoes with ham spread and walnuts
(Illustrated on page 47)

Omit the cucumber and chives and garnish instead with walnut halves and parsley.

Kohlrabi spread

4 small kohlrabi, peeled
40 g/1½ oz butter
150 g/5 oz curd cheese or quark
salt
paprika
1–2 tablespoons milk (optional)

Finely grate the kohlrabi. Cream the butter with the curd cheese or quark and stir in the grated kohlrabi. Season to taste with salt and paprika. If the mixture is too thick, add a little milk.

Kohlrabi stuffed with vegetable salad
(Illustrated on page 46)

4 small kohlrabi
2 tablespoons natural yogurt
1 tablespoon mayonnaise
50 g/2 oz cocktail onions, chopped
½ green pepper, deseeded and chopped
1 tomato, deseeded and chopped
4 radishes, chopped
salt and freshly ground white pepper
2 large button mushrooms to garnish

Peel the kohlrabi and scoop out the centres. Blanch for 2–3 minutes in boiling water, drain and cool. Mix the yogurt and mayonnaise together in a bowl, add the cocktail onions, green pepper, tomato and radish. Season with salt and pepper and toss the salad gently. Spoon into the kohlrabi shells. Wipe the mushrooms and cut into thick slices to garnish.

Kohlrabi stuffed with savoury salad
(Illustrated on page 47)

4 small kohlrabi
3 tablespoons natural yogurt
2 tablespoons mayonnaise
25 g/1 oz capers
½ red pepper, deseeded and chopped
50 g/2 oz cucumber, chopped
salt and freshly ground white pepper
Garnish:
    4 gherkins
    extra capers

Peel the kohlrabi and scoop out the insides. Blanch for 2–3 minutes in boiling water, drain and cool. Mix together the yogurt and mayonnaise and stir in the capers, pepper and cucumber. Season to taste with salt and pepper. Toss gently and pile into the kohlrabi shells. Garnish with gherkins and the extra capers.

Cucumber with cream cheese and radish
(Illustrated on page 47)

225 g/8 oz cucumber, peeled
75 g/3 oz butter
75 g/3 oz cream cheese
salt
4 radishes
extra cucumber to garnish

Cut the cucumber into four equal pieces. Scoop out slightly. Cream the butter with the cream cheese and season to taste with salt. Use this mixture to fill the cucumbers. Top with slices of radish and extra slices or balls of cucumber.

Mixed vegetable cocktail

150 g/5 oz canned asparagus, chopped
75 g/3 oz cooked peas
75 g/3 oz cocktail onions
75 g/3 oz cooked carrots, diced
75 g/3 oz button mushrooms, sliced
2 tablespoons mayonnaise
2 tablespoons double cream
1 tablespoon concentrated tomato purée
salt and freshly ground black pepper
1–2 teaspoons lemon juice
chopped chives to garnish

Mix together the vegetables and divide between four glasses. Mix together the mayonnaise, double cream and tomato purée and season to taste with salt, pepper and lemon juice. Pour the dressing over the vegetables and garnish with chopped chives.

Crispbread with herb spread

(Illustrated on page 47)

75 g/3 oz butter
75 g/3 oz cream or curd cheese
salt and freshly ground black pepper
3 tablespoons chopped fresh mixed herbs (for example parsley, dill, basil, tarragon)
4 pieces crispbread
4 spring onions to garnish

Cream the butter with the cheese and season to taste with salt and pepper. Mix in the herbs. Spread the mixture on the crispbread. Slice the white part of the spring onions and chop the green part and use to garnish the crispbreads.

VEGETABLE OPEN SANDWICHES

Tomato and olive

(Illustrated on page 47)

4 slices of white bread or bought toast
butter for spreading
225 g/8 oz tomatoes, sliced
salt

Garnish:
4 black olives
4 rings raw onion

Spread the bread with butter and arrange the sliced tomatoes on top. Sprinkle with salt and garnish with a black olive and an onion ring.

Garlic butter

(Illustrated on page 47)

4 slices of white bread
75 g/3 oz butter
1 fat clove garlic
salt and freshly ground white pepper
1–2 teaspoons lemon juice
Garnish:
lettuce leaves
1 hard-boiled egg, sliced

Cream the butter until soft. Peel and crush the garlic and beat into the butter. Season to taste with salt, pepper and lemon juice. Spread the bread with the butter and garnish with a lettuce leaf and slices of the hard-boiled egg.

Radish

(Illustrated on page 47)

4 slices of white bread or bought toast
butter for spreading
small bunch radishes, sliced
salt and freshly ground white pepper
parsley sprigs to garnish

Spread the bread with butter and top with radishes. Sprinkle with salt and pepper to taste and garnish with a sprig of parsley.

Kohlrabi

(Illustrated on page 47)

50 g/2 oz butter
50 g/2 oz Cheddar cheese, grated
4 slices of white bread or bought toast
75 g/3 oz kohlrabi
4 chillies to garnish

Cream the butter and mix with the cheese. Spread this mixture on the bread. Finely grate the kohlrabi and pile on top of the cheese mixture. Garnish with the chillies.

Iced piquant vegetable soup, Chinese ▶ vegetable soup, Chilled cucumber soup
Cream of onion soup, Cream of spinach soup, Beetroot soup
Spring vegetable soup

Soups

Chinese vegetable soup

(Illustrated on page 50)

50 g/2 oz dried Chinese mushrooms,
   soaked in warm water for
   20 minutes
1 large carrot
75 g/3 oz canned bamboo shoots
2 sticks celery
75 g/3 oz French beans
750 ml/1¼ pints chicken stock
salt and freshly ground black pepper
1–2 tablespoons soy sauce

Cut all the vegetables into thin strips or decorative shapes. Bring the stock to the boil in a saucepan and add the vegetables. Bring back to the boil rapidly and cook until the vegetables are tender. Remove from the heat and add salt, pepper and soy sauce to taste.

Cream of onion soup

(Illustrated on page 51)

3 large onions, finely chopped
75 g/3 oz butter
50 g/2 oz plain flour
750 ml/1¼ pints chicken stock
salt and freshly ground black pepper
2 egg yolks

3 tablespoons double cream
fried onion rings to garnish

Fry the onion gently in the butter until soft and transparent. Do not allow to brown. Stir in the flour and cook briefly. Add the stock, bring to the boil, then reduce the heat and simmer gently for 20 minutes. Add salt and pepper to taste. Pass the mixture through a sieve. Return to the saucepan and heat through. Mix together the egg yolks and cream and stir into the soup. Serve immediately, garnished with fried onion rings.

Iced piquant vegetable soup

(Illustrated on page 50)

100 ml/4 fl oz natural yogurt
100 ml/4 fl oz single cream
300 ml/½ pint vegetable or chicken
   stock
1 tablespoon mild prepared mustard
salt and freshly ground black pepper
1–2 teaspoons vinegar or lemon juice
1–2 teaspoons caster sugar
100 g/4 oz cucumber, grated
2 tomatoes, peeled and chopped

1 small red or green pepper,
   deseeded and chopped
75 g/3 oz spring onions, finely
   chopped
chopped chives to garnish

Combine the yogurt, cream, stock and mustard and season to taste with salt, pepper, vinegar or lemon juice and sugar. Mix well. Add the cucumber, tomato, pepper and spring onion. Stir and chill. If the soup is too thick, add a few ice cubes. Garnish with chopped chives.

Chilled cucumber soup

(Illustrated on page 50)

450 ml/¾ pint milk
250 ml/8 fl oz double cream
3 cloves garlic, peeled and crushed
salt and freshly ground black pepper
1–2 teaspoons vinegar
1 large cucumber
2 tablespoons chopped fresh dill or
   mint
extra strips cucumber to garnish

Mix the milk with the double cream, add the garlic and season with salt, pepper and vinegar. Peel the cucumber, cut into fine strips or grate coarsely and stir into the mixture. Chill well. Just before serving stir in the dill or mint and garnish with strips of cucumber.

Spring vegetable soup
(Illustrated on page 51)

25 g/1 oz butter
1 medium carrot, cut into strips
50 g/2 oz frozen or fresh peas
1 small kohlrabi, diced
75 g/3 oz baby corn cobs, halved, or
    75 g/3 oz frozen sweetcorn
50 g/2 oz cauliflower florets
50 g/2 oz button mushrooms, wiped
    and sliced
750 ml/1¼ pints beef or chicken
    stock
salt and freshly ground black pepper
2 eggs, lightly beaten
2 tablespoons chopped parsley to
    garnish

Melt the butter in a large saucepan and add the vegetables. Stir to coat with butter, then cover with a lid and leave to cook very gently for 10 minutes or until just beginning to soften. Add the stock and bring to the boil. Reduce the heat and simmer gently for 20 minutes. Season to taste with salt and pepper. Stir in the eggs and serve immediately, garnished with chopped parsley.

Beetroot soup
(Illustrated on page 51)

225 g/8 oz stewing beef

750 ml/1¼ pints water
salt and black peppercorns
225 g/8 oz cooked beetroot
Garnish (optional):
    extra beetroot and slices of other
    cooked root vegetables
    (e.g. carrot, parsnip)
    4 egg yolks
    4 sprigs parsley

Cut the beef into 1-cm/½-in cubes. Put it in a saucepan with the cold water, salt to taste and a few peppercorns. Bring to the boil and simmer gently for 1–1½ hours or until the beef is tender. Grate the beetroot and add to the soup. Discard the peppercorns. Simmer for a further 10–15 minutes. For the garnish, cut the beetroot and other vegetables into decorative shapes, and have the egg yolks ready. Pour the piping hot soup into four serving bowls, add the slices of vegetable and an egg yolk to each bowl. Finally top with a sprig of parsley and serve immediately.

Cream of spinach soup
(Illustrated on page 51)

50 g/2 oz butter
40 g/1½ oz plain flour
600 ml/1 pint beef stock
salt and freshly ground black pepper
1 (227-g/8-oz) packet frozen spinach
300 ml/½ pint milk
100 ml/4 fl oz double cream
2 egg yolks

Garnish:
    1 hard-boiled egg, chopped
    paprika

Melt the butter in a saucepan and stir in the flour. Cook for a few minutes. Add the stock and seasoning to taste. Bring to the boil, stirring all the time, and simmer for about 10 minutes. Add the frozen spinach and milk and bring back to the boil. Simmer for a further 10 minutes or until the block of spinach is completely thawed. Mix together the cream and egg yolks and stir into the soup. Remove from the heat and pour into individual bowls. Serve at once, garnished with chopped hard-boiled egg and a sprinkling of paprika.

Czech mountain soup
(Illustrated on page 54)

225 g/8 oz canned or bottled sauer-
    kraut
1 large potato, peeled and diced
1 large onion, chopped
50 g/2 oz butter
40 g/1½ oz plain flour
600 ml/1 pint milk
150 ml/¼ pint single cream
salt and freshly ground black pepper
1 teaspoon caraway seeds
1 tablespoon chopped chives

Rinse the sauerkraut and place it in a saucepan with the diced potato. Pour over boiling water to cover and simmer gently for 30 minutes

or until soft. Fry the onion in the butter until soft but not browned then stir in the flour. Add the milk, stir well and bring to the boil. Cook for a few minutes. Add the sauerkraut and potato and stir in the cream. Season to taste with salt and pepper. Sprinkle with caraway seeds and chives just before serving. Serve with crusty bread for a warming winter dish.

◄ *Scotch broth, Czech mountain soup Garlic soup*

Sauerkraut soup with garlic sausage, Gardeners' soup, French bean soup with soured cream ►

Garlic soup

(Illustrated on page 54)

50 g/2 oz dripping or hard vegetable
  fat
1 small celeriac, diced
450 g/1 lb potatoes, diced
750 ml/1¼ pints water
4 cloves garlic, crushed
salt and freshly ground black pepper
Garnish:
  chopped spring onions
  croûtons

Melt the fat in a large saucepan and
fry the celeriac until just beginning
to soften. Add the potatoes and
water and simmer gently for 20 minutes or until the vegetables are soft.
Crush the garlic. Mix the garlic
with salt and add to the soup.
Season with pepper. Serve sprinkled
with chopped spring onions and
hand the croûtons separately.

Gardeners' soup

(Illustrated on page 55)

50 g/2 oz carrots, diced
50 g/2 oz celeriac, diced
50 g/2 oz cauliflower florets
50 g/2 oz Savoy cabbage, chopped
750 ml/1¼ pints beef, chicken, or
  vegetable stock
75 g/3 oz butter
40 g/1½ oz plain flour
salt and freshly ground black pepper
pinch ground mace
50 g/2 oz canned asparagus, sliced

50 g/2 oz frozen peas
100 ml/4 fl oz double cream
2 egg yolks
chopped parsley to garnish

Put the carrot, celeriac, cauliflower
and cabbage into a saucepan, pour
over half the stock and bring to the
boil, then simmer for 20 minutes.
Melt the butter and stir in the flour.
Cook for a few minutes. Add salt
and pepper to taste and the mace.
Add the rest of the stock, bring to
the boil and simmer for 5 minutes.
Add the cooked vegetables with
their cooking liquid, asparagus and
peas. Simmer for a further 5 minutes.
Mix the cream with the egg yolks
and add to the soup. Remove from
the heat and serve immediately,
garnished with chopped parsley.

Sauerkraut soup
with garlic sausage

(Illustrated on page 55)

150 g/5 oz canned or bottled sauerkraut
40 g/1½ oz dripping
1 small onion, chopped
40 g/1½ oz plain flour
salt and freshly ground black pepper
1 teaspoon caraway seeds
750 ml/1¼ pints beef stock
100 g/4 oz garlic sausage
40 g/1½ oz butter
100 ml/4 fl oz soured cream

Rinse the sauerkraut well, then place
in a pan with 300 ml/½ pint water.
Bring to the boil and simmer for

30 minutes. Meanwhile melt the
dripping in a large saucepan and
fry the onion until soft. Stir in the
flour and cook until it is lightly
browned. Add salt and pepper to
taste and the caraway seeds. Pour
over the stock, bring to the boil
and simmer for 5–10 minutes. Add
the sauerkraut with its cooking
liquid. Slice the sausage and fry
in butter until lightly browned. Add
to the soup. Swirl in the soured
cream, remove from the heat and
serve immediately.

French bean soup
with soured cream

(Illustrated on page 55)

50 g/2 oz dripping
2 small onions, chopped
40 g/1½ oz plain flour
600 ml/1 pint beef stock
600 ml/1 pint milk
150 g/5 oz French beans, cut into
  2.5-cm/1-in slices
2 tablespoons soured cream
50 g/2 oz streaky bacon, derinded
  and chopped
100 g/4 oz garlic sausage
1 teaspoon paprika
salt
dash vinegar

Melt the dripping in a large saucepan and fry the onion until soft
but not browned. Stir in the flour,
add the stock and milk. Bring to
the boil, add the beans and simmer
for about 20 minutes or until the

beans are soft. Stir in the soured cream. Fry the bacon in a small pan until the fat runs, add the garlic sausage and fry until browned. Pour the mixture over the soup. Add the paprika, salt to taste and a dash of vinegar. Serve immediately.

Scotch broth

(Illustrated on page 54)

1 small celeriac
2 large carrots
100 g/4 oz Brussels sprouts
50 g/2 oz pearl barley
750 ml/1¼ pints beef or lamb stock
salt and freshly ground black pepper

Cut the celeriac and carrots into thin strips and place in a large saucepan with the Brussels sprouts, barley and stock. Bring to the boil, then reduce the heat and simmer for about 1 hour or until the vegetables and barley are tender. Season to taste before serving.

Bean soup with pasta

(Illustrated on page 59)

40 g/1½ oz dripping or hard vegetable fat
1 medium onion, chopped
50 g/2 oz plain flour
750 ml/1¼ pints beef or chicken stock
225 g/8 oz runner beans, sliced
75 g/3 oz pasta shapes
salt and freshly ground black pepper

1 tablespoon chopped parsley to garnish

Melt the fat and fry the onion until soft but not browned. Stir in the flour and fry for a further 2 minutes. Add the stock, bring to the boil and simmer for about 5 minutes. Add the beans and the pasta shapes and simmer for a further 15 minutes or until the beans are soft. Season to taste with salt and pepper. Pour into serving bowls and sprinkle over the parsley.

Sauerkraut soup with mushrooms

(Illustrated on page 59)

225 g/8 oz canned or bottled sauer-kraut, rinsed
1 large potato, diced
1 bay leaf
750 ml/1¼ pints water
75 g/3 oz streaky bacon, derinded and chopped
1 large onion, diced
button mushrooms, sliced
salt and freshly ground black pepper
100 ml/4 fl oz single cream

Put the rinsed sauerkraut, potato and bay leaf in a large saucepan and pour over the water. Bring to the boil and simmer for 30 minutes or until the vegetables are tender. Discard the bay leaf. In another pan fry the bacon until the fat runs. Add the onion and cook gently until soft. Add the mushrooms and fry gently for a further five minutes.

Combine with the cooked sauer-kraut mixture and heat through thoroughly. Season to taste with salt and pepper and swirl in the cream just before serving.

Onion soup with meat and mushrooms

(Illustrated on page 59)

175 g/6 oz button mushrooms, sliced
2 large onions, chopped
4 tablespoons oil
750 ml/1¼ pints beef stock
salt and freshly ground black pepper
175 g/6 oz boiled potatoes, diced
100 g/4 oz cooked beef, diced
4 sprigs parsley to garnish

Fry the mushroom and onion gently in the oil until the onion is soft but not browned. Add the stock, bring to the boil and simmer for 20 minutes. Add salt and pepper to taste and the diced potatoes and meat. Heat through thoroughly and pour into serving bowls. Garnish each bowl with a sprig of parsley.

Savoy cabbage soup with potatoes, ▶
Sauerkraut soup with fish

Bean soup with pasta, Sauerkraut soup with mushrooms

Onion soup with meat and mushrooms, Cream of bean soup

Savoy cabbage soup with potatoes

(Illustrated on page 58)

75 g/3 oz dripping or hard vegetable
    fat
1 medium onion, chopped
1 clove garlic, crushed
1 teaspoon caraway seeds
40 g/1½ oz plain flour
750 ml/1¼ pints beef stock
175 g/6 oz potatoes, diced
1 teaspoon dried marjoram
225 g/8 oz Savoy cabbage, shredded
salt and freshly ground black pepper
1 tablespoon chopped parsley to
    garnish

Melt the fat in a large saucepan
and stir in the onion. Fry until soft
but not browned. Add the garlic
and caraway seeds and fry for
a further minute. Stir in the flour
and continue cooking for 2 minutes.
Pour over the stock, bring to the
boil, then simmer gently for
5 minutes. Add the diced potatoes
and the marjoram and cook until
the potatoes are just soft (about
15 minutes). Then add the Savoy
cabbage and cook for a further
10–15 minutes or until soft. Season
with salt and pepper to taste. Garnish
each portion with chopped parsley.

Cream of bean soup

(Illustrated on page 59)

50 g/2 oz butter

2 small onions, chopped
40 g/1½ oz plain flour
750 ml/1¼ pints beef or vegetable
    stock
salt and freshly ground black pepper
225 g/8 oz potatoes, diced
225 g/8 oz runner or French beans,
    chopped
100 ml/4 fl oz single cream
2 egg yolks
dash vinegar
1 tablespoon chopped parsley to
    garnish

Melt the butter in a large saucepan
and fry the onion until soft but
not browned. Stir in the flour and
cook for a further minute. Add the
stock and bring to the boil, stirring
frequently. Simmer for 5 minutes.
Season to taste with salt and pepper,
then add the potatoes and beans.
Simmer for a further 25 minutes or
until the vegetables are tender. Mix
together the cream and egg yolks
and stir into the soup. Add a dash
of vinegar. Pour into serving bowls
and sprinkle with chopped parsley.

Savoy cabbage soup with rice

40 g/1½ oz butter
40 g/1½ oz plain flour
750 ml/1¼ pints beef stock
salt and freshly ground black pepper
25 g/1 oz rice
175 g/6 oz Savoy cabbage, shredded
2 egg yolks

250 ml/8 fl oz milk
1 tablespoon chopped chives to
    garnish

Melt the butter in a large pan and
stir in the flour. Cook for 1 to
2 minutes. Add the stock and
seasoning to taste. Bring to the
boil and simmer for 10 minutes.
Meanwhile cook the rice in a small
quantity of boiling water until tender
and blanch the cabbage in boiling
water for 3 minutes. Drain the rice
and cabbage and place in a warmed
tureen. Mix the egg yolks with the
milk and add to the stock. Adjust
the seasoning, then strain over the
cabbage and the rice. Sprinkle with
chopped chives and serve immediately.

Chilled tomato soup

450 ml/¾ pint tomato juice
100 ml/4 fl oz single cream
225 g/8 oz tomatoes, peeled,
    deseeded and chopped
1 medium onion, finely chopped
1 tablespoon chopped chives
salt and freshly ground black pepper
4 ice cubes to garnish

Combine the tomato juice and cream
in a bowl. Stir in the tomato, onion
and chives and season to taste with
salt and pepper. Chill well. Just
before serving pour into individual
bowls and float an ice cube in each
one.

Onion soup
with cheese toasts

100 g/4 oz butter
3 large onions, sliced into rings
40 g/1½ oz plain flour
750 ml/1¼ pints beef stock
salt and freshly ground black pepper
4 slices toast
75 g/3 oz Cheddar cheese, grated
1 tablespoon chopped parsley to
    garnish

Melt the butter in a large saucepan
and fry the onion rings until just
beginning to colour. Stir in the
flour and add the stock, then salt
and pepper to taste. Bring to the
boil, then simmer for 20 minutes.
Cut the toast into small squares or
triangles. Heat the grill to its hottest
setting. Pour the soup into flameproof bowls and add the pieces of
toast. Sprinkle over the grated cheese
and place under the grill until the
cheese is bubbling and golden.
Sprinkle with chopped parsley and
serve immediately.

Cream of lettuce soup

75 g/3 oz butter
40 g/1½ oz plain flour
750 ml/1¼ pints beef or vegetable
    stock
1 large head lettuce, chopped
100 ml/4 fl oz single cream or milk
salt
freshly grated nutmeg

Melt the butter and stir in the flour.
Cook for a few minutes, add the
stock and cook for 10 minutes. Stir
in the finely chopped lettuce and
the cream, season with salt and
grated nutmeg. Serve with poached
eggs, if desired.

Tomato soup
with chicken

40 g/1½ oz butter
1 small onion, chopped
40 g/1½ oz plain flour
300 ml/½ pint chicken stock
300 ml/½ pint tomato juice
salt and freshly ground black pepper
175 g/6 oz cooked chicken, diced
225 g/8 oz tomatoes, peeled,
    deseeded and chopped
100 ml/4 fl oz single cream
2 tablespoons chopped parsley to
    garnish

Melt the butter in a large saucepan
and fry the onion until soft. Sprinkle
over the flour and cook for a further
2 minutes stirring all the time. Pour
over the stock and tomato juice,
bring to the boil and simmer for
10 minutes. Strain the soup into
a clean saucepan and season to
taste. Add the chicken and chopped
tomato and heat through gently.
Remove from the heat and stir in
the cream. Serve immediately, garnished with chopped parsley.

Chicken
and sweetcorn soup

40 g/1½ oz butter
40 g/1½ oz plain flour
600 ml/1 pint chicken stock
salt and freshly ground white pepper
225 g/8 oz fresh or frozen sweetcorn
225 g/8 oz cooked chicken breast,
    diced
100 ml/4 fl oz double cream
2 egg yolks
2 tablespoons chopped parsley to
    garnish

Melt the butter in a large saucepan
and stir in the flour. Cook for
2 minutes. Add the chicken stock
and bring to the boil. Simmer for
5 minutes. Season to taste with salt
and pepper, then add the sweetcorn.
Simmer for a further 10 minutes.
Add the chicken and heat through
thoroughly. Mix the cream with the
egg yolks and stir into the soup.
Serve immediately, garnished with
chopped parsley.

Main dishes and accompaniments

Broccoli dumplings

(Illustrated on page 62)

450 g/1 lb broccoli
4 eggs, separated
150 g/5 oz cooked semolina
pinch ground mace
salt
oil for frying

Cook the broccoli in salted water for 10–15 minutes or until tender. Chop it and mix with the egg yolks, semolina, mace and salt to taste. Whisk the egg whites until they form soft peaks, then fold into the broccoli mixture. Heat the oil in a frying pan and drop spoonfuls of the mixture in. Cook for about 10 minutes or until golden brown on all sides and cooked through.

Baked aubergine with egg

(Illustrated on page 63)

2 large aubergines
40 g/1½ oz butter

◀ *Broccoli dumplings and croquettes*
Baked aubergine with egg

1 tablespoon chopped chives
salt and freshly ground black pepper
75 g/3 oz streaky bacon
4 eggs
black olives to garnish

Cut the aubergines in half and trim off the rounded ends. Scoop out the flesh and reserve. Blanch the outside shells for 2–3 minutes in boiling water, then peel off the skins. Chop the scooped-out aubergine flesh. Melt the butter in a saucepan. Add the chives and salt and pepper to taste. Cover the saucepan with a lid and cook over a low heat for 20–30 minutes or until the aubergine is soft. Arrange the four aubergine shells in an ovenproof dish and line with rashers of bacon. Pile on the cooked aubergine and break an egg into each shell. Bake in a moderate oven (180 C, 350 F, gas 4) for some 30 minutes or until the aubergine shells are tender. Garnish each portion with a black olive just before serving.

Broccoli croquettes

(Illustrated on page 62)

450 g/1 lb broccoli

1 small onion, chopped
40 g/1½ oz butter
100 g/4 oz Cheddar cheese, grated
75 g/3 oz dry breadcrumbs
2 eggs, beaten
salt
oil for frying
lemon wedges for serving

Cook the broccoli in salted water for 10–15 minutes or until tender. Drain and chop finely. Fry the chopped onion in the butter until just beginning to brown. Add the broccoli, grated cheese, 50 g/2 oz of the breadcrumbs and eggs. Season to taste with salt. Form balls or flat cakes from this mixture, dip them in the remaining breadcrumbs and shallow fry in hot oil for 10 minutes, turning once. Garnish with lemon wedges and serve with boiled potatoes and a cold savoury sauce.

Broccoli with ham

450 g/1 lb broccoli
75 g/3 oz streaky bacon
2 leeks, sliced
salt and freshly ground black pepper
225 g/8 oz cooked ham, chopped

Wash the broccoli, cook it in boiling salted water for 10 minutes and drain. Chop the bacon and fry until the fat runs. Add the leeks and season to taste with salt and pepper. Cook gently for about 5 minutes. Stir in the ham and continue cooking to heat through thoroughly. Put the broccoli in a serving dish and top with the ham mixture. Serve with potatoes or as an accompaniment to roast or boiled pork, beef or mutton.

Bulgarian vegetable hotpot

(Illustrated on page 66)

4 tablespoons oil
1 large onion, sliced
1 clove garlic, crushed
225 g/8 oz red or green peppers, deseeded and cut into rings
225 g/8 oz tomatoes, peeled and chopped
50 g/2 oz black olives, stoned
3 tablespoons white wine
salt
paprika
chopped spring onion to garnish

Heat the oil in a large frying pan and fry the onion and garlic until just softened. Add the peppers, tomato, olives and wine. Simmer for 10 minutes and season to taste with salt and paprika. Garnish with chopped spring onion and serve with grilled meat and a plain steamed vegetable such as courgette or marrow.

Baked leeks with ham

(Illustrated on page 67)

4 large leeks
4 (50-g/2-oz) slices cooked ham
100 g/4 oz button mushrooms
40 g/1½ oz butter
salt and freshly ground black pepper
dill or parsley sprigs to garnish

Trim the leeks and wash well. Blanch in boiling salted water for 5 minutes. Drain. Place each leek on a slice of ham and roll up the ham. Reserve 4 small mushrooms for the garnish and chop the rest. Use half the butter to grease an ovenproof dish and line with the chopped mushrooms. Lay the leek and ham rolls on top of the mushrooms. Add a good seasoning of salt and pepper and dot with the remaining butter. Finally top each leek with a reserved mushroom. Bake in a moderate oven (180 C, 350 F, gas 4) for 25–30 minutes, until tender and browned. Garnish with sprigs of dill or parsley before serving.

Savoy cabbage rolls with meat filling

(Illustrated on page 66)

1 medium onion, finely chopped
1 clove garlic, crushed
350 g/12 oz beef or pork mince
salt and freshly ground black pepper
4 large leaves of Savoy cabbage
4 thin slices cooked ham
150 ml/¼ pint beef stock

Mix the onion and garlic with the meat and season with salt and pepper. Mix well. Blanch the cabbage leaves in boiling salted water for 2 minutes and drain. Slightly crush the thick ribs with a meat hammer or the back of a wooden spoon. Divide the meat mixture evenly between the leaves and roll them up, tucking in the ends neatly. Then roll each leaf in a slice of ham. Place the rolls in a greased ovenproof dish, pour over the stock, cover with a lid and braise for 1 hour in a moderately hot oven (190 C, 175 F, gas 5). About 15 minutes before the end of the cooking time remove the lid to allow the rolls to brown a little. Serve with boiled or fried potatoes and baked tomatoes.

Broccoli with herb butter

450 g/1 lb broccoli
4 lemon wedges
75 g/3 oz herb butter (see page 201)
salt and freshly ground black pepper

Cook the broccoli in boiling salted water for about 10 minutes or until just tender. Top each portion with a wedge of lemon and a slice of herb butter. Season lightly with salt and freshly ground pepper.

Bulgarian vegetable hotpot

Savoy cabbage rolls with meat filling

Baked leeks with ham ▶

Aubergines with piquant sauce

2 medium aubergines
oil for frying
2 tablespoons plain flour
1 egg, beaten
2 tablespoons dry breadcrumbs
Sauce:
3 cloves garlic, crushed
2 shallots, finely chopped
2 tablespoons oil
salt and white pepper to taste
1 tablespoon lemon juice
1–2 tablespoons chopped dill or parsley

Cut the aubergines into 1-cm/$\frac{1}{2}$-in slices. Heat the oil in the frying pan. Dip the slices first into flour, then into the beaten egg and breadcrumbs and fry, a few at a time, over medium heat until golden on both sides and cooked through. Add more oil to the pan as necessary and keep the cooked slices warm. Combine the sauce ingredients together in a screw-topped jar and shake until well mixed. Pile the aubergines on to a warmed serving dish and hand the sauce separately.

Fried vegetable turnovers

Dough:
450 g/1 lb plain flour
generous pinch salt
15 g/$\frac{1}{2}$ oz dried yeast
150 ml/$\frac{1}{4}$ pint lukewarm milk

1 teaspoon sugar
40 g/1$\frac{1}{2}$ oz butter
1 egg
Filling:
1 small onion, chopped
40 g/1$\frac{1}{2}$ oz lard
100 g/4 oz cabbage, shredded
salt and freshly ground black pepper
2 eggs, beaten
40 g/1$\frac{1}{2}$ oz carrots, grated
50 g/2 oz ham, diced
oil for frying

First make the dough by sifting the flour and salt together in a large bowl. Dissolve the dried yeast in the milk with the sugar and leave for 10 minutes or until frothy. Melt the butter. Mix the yeast, butter and egg into the flour and knead until smooth and elastic. Roll out the dough into a square measuring 42 cm/18 in and cut that into six 7-cm/3-in squares. For the filling fry the onion in the lard. Add the cabbage, seasoning to taste and fry gently until soft. Pour the beaten eggs over and cook for a few minutes. Cool and fold in the carrots and ham. Fill the squares of dough with this mixture, pressing down the turned-over edges. Fry until golden brown, about 2 minutes on each side.

Baked vegetables with eggs

4 tablespoons oil
2 large onions, chopped
100 g/4 oz carrots, diced

100 g/4 oz celeriac, diced
225 g/8 oz potatoes, diced
3 tablespoons concentrated tomato purée
1 small red or green pepper, deseeded and chopped
100 g/4 oz frozen or fresh peas
2 tomatoes, quartered
8 rashers bacon
150 ml/$\frac{1}{4}$ pint milk
5 eggs
salt and freshly ground black pepper
1 tablespoon chopped parsley

Heat the oil in a saucepan and fry the onion over low heat until soft. Add the carrots and celeriac and continue to fry for a few minutes. Add the potatoes and tomato purée, cover and simmer very gently for 15–20 minutes or until the vegetables are tender. Add the pepper, peas and tomatoes and stew for a further 5 minutes. Line four individual ovenproof dishes with the bacon rashers and divide the vegetable mixture evenly between them. Mix together the milk and eggs and season with salt and pepper. Pour the egg mixture over the vegetables and sprinkle with parsley. Bake in a moderately hot oven (200 C, 400 F, gas 6) for 30–40 minutes.

Broccoli with almonds

450 g/1 lb broccoli
50 g/2 oz blanched almonds

75 g/3 oz butter
40 g/1½ oz dry breadcrumbs
salt and freshly ground white pepper

Cook the broccoli in boiling salted water for about 10 minutes or until just tender. Slice the blanched almonds lengthways. Melt the butter in a frying pan and toss the almonds for a few minutes. Add the dry breadcrumbs, salt and pepper and continue frying until golden brown. Place the broccoli in a warmed serving dish and top with the almond mixture.

Savoy cabbage with mushrooms

(Illustrated on page 70)

1 medium Savoy cabbage
75 g/3 oz streaky bacon, derinded
 · and chopped
1 small onion, chopped
225 g/8 oz mushrooms, sliced
salt and freshly ground black pepper
1–2 teaspoons caraway seeds
225 g/8 oz cooked rice
4 eggs, lightly beaten
25 g/1 oz butter
50 g/2 oz Emmental cheese, grated
Garnish :
    tomato slices
    4 sprigs parsley

Shred the cabbage, blanch for 2 minutes in boiling salted water, then drain. Fry the bacon until the fat runs, then add the onion and

cook gently until soft. Stir in the mushrooms with seasoning and caraway seeds to taste and cook until the juice runs from the mushrooms. Add the cabbage, rice and eggs and mix well. Grease four individual ovenproof dishes with the butter and divide the mixture evenly between them. Bake in a moderately hot oven (200 C, 400 F, gas 6) for 8–10 minutes. Scatter the grated cheese on top and continue baking for a further 10 minutes until the top is golden brown. Garnish with slices of tomato and sprigs of parsley.

Broccoli with garlic

450 g/1 lb broccoli
75 g/3 oz streaky bacon, chopped
1 medium onion, chopped
3 cloves garlic, crushed
salt and freshly ground black pepper
150 ml/¼ pint beef stock or water

Blanch the broccoli for 2 minutes in boiling salted water and drain. Fry the bacon in a saucepan until the fat runs. Add the onion and fry until soft but not browned. Stir in the garlic and fry for a further minute. Add the broccoli and season to taste with salt and pepper. Add the stock and cover the pan with a lid. Cook gently for 10–15 minutes or until the broccoli is just tender. Serve as a main dish with potatoes or as an accompaniment to beef or lamb.

Bulgarian sarma

(Illustrated on page 70)

450 g/1 lb beef, pork or lamb mince
100 g/4 oz cooked rice
1 egg
1 large onion, finely chopped
salt and freshly ground black pepper
paprika
8 large cabbage leaves
2 tablespoons oil
225 g/8 oz canned or bottled sauerkraut, rinsed
3 tablespoons concentrated tomato purée
100 ml/4 fl oz soured cream or natural yogurt
1 tablespoon chopped parsley to garnish

Mix together the mince, rice, egg and half the onion and season with salt, pepper and paprika. Blanch the cabbage leaves for 2 minutes, then drain. Divide the meat mixture evenly between the cabbage leaves and roll up to make neat parcels. Heat the oil in a saucepan and fry the rest of the onion. Add the rinsed sauerkraut and tomato purée and cook gently for 15 minutes. Turn the sauerkraut mixture into a greased ovenproof dish and top with the cabbage rolls. Cover and bake for 40 minutes in a moderately hot oven (190 C, 375 F, gas 5) for 40 minutes. Pour over the soured cream or yogurt 15 minutes before the end of the cooking time. Sprinkle with chopped parsley just before serving.

Bulgarian sarma

Savoy cabbage with mushrooms

Broccoli and tomato bake ▶

Broccoli and tomato bake

(Illustrated on page 71)

450 g/1 lb broccoli
50 g/2 oz butter
100 g/4 oz cooked ham, chopped
2 large tomatoes, chopped
salt and freshly ground black pepper

Cook the broccoli in boiling salted water for 10 minutes or until just tender and drain well. Arrange half of it in an ovenproof dish greased with half the butter. Mix together the ham and tomato and season with pepper and extra salt, if desired. Cover with the rest of the broccoli and dot with the remaining butter. Bake in a moderately hot oven (200 C, 400 F, gas 6) for 10–15 minutes or until piping hot and just beginning to colour.

Asparagus with herb butter

450 g/1 lb fresh asparagus
100 g/4 oz herb butter (see page 201)
4 lemon wedges
4 sprigs parsley

Wash and trim the asparagus. Steam or cook in a sparing amount of boiling salted water for 10–15 minutes, until just tender. Drain and arrange on four warmed serving plates. Top each portion with a slice of herb butter, a wedge of lemon and a sprig of parsley.

Broccoli with pine nuts

450 g/1 lb broccoli
75 g/3 oz butter
75 g/3 oz pine nuts
75 g/3 oz cooked ham, chopped
salt and freshly ground black pepper
1 tablespoon chopped chives

Cook the broccoli in boiling salted water for 10 minutes or until just done. Drain and place in a warmed serving dish. Melt the butter in a frying pan and add the pine nuts and ham with a seasoning of pepper and extra salt, if desired. Fry until golden, then pour over the broccoli and serve at once.

Vegetable burgers with mushrooms

40 g/1½ oz butter
40 g/1½ oz plain flour
3 tablespoons milk
salt and freshly ground black pepper
pinch ground mace
50 g/2 oz fresh white breadcrumbs
2 eggs, lightly beaten
225 g/8 oz cooked vegetables, finely chopped
100 g/4 oz mushrooms, finely chopped
4 tablespoons oil
dried breadcrumbs for coating

Melt the butter, stir in the flour. Cook for 1–2 minutes over a low heat. Add the milk and continue cooking until the mixture thickens. Season to taste with salt, pepper and mace. Cool and mix in the fresh breadcrumbs and eggs. Fold in the cooked vegetables and mushrooms. Form small burgers and coat them with dried breadcrumbs. Heat the oil in a frying pan and fry the burgers for 10 minutes, turning once. Serve with potatoes and a crisp green salad.

Pasta and vegetable bake

225 g/8 oz pasta shapes
350 g/12 oz cooked mixed vegetables
butter for greasing
3 eggs
300 ml/½ pint single cream or creamy milk
salt and freshly ground black pepper
pinch ground mace
1 tablespoon chopped parsley

Cook the pasta according to the directions on the packet, rinse in cold water and drain well. Mix with the vegetables. Grease an ovenproof dish generously with butter and fill with the pasta mixture. Mix together the eggs and cream and season well with salt, pepper and mace. Pour this mixture over the pasta and bake in a moderate oven (180 C, 350 F, gas 4) for 35–40 minutes or until set and golden brown. Sprinkle with parsley before serving. This goes well with cucumber salad dressed with soured cream.

Meat and vegetable burgers

225 g/8 oz minced beef or pork
50 g/2 oz fresh white breadcrumbs
1 egg
25 g/1 oz plain flour
salt and freshly ground black pepper
pinch ground mace
225 g/8 oz cooked vegetables, finely
    chopped
2 tablespoons oil

Mix the mince with the breadcrumbs, egg and flour and season well with salt, pepper and mace. Add the cooked vegetables and mix well. Divide the mixture into eight portions and form into flat burger shapes. Heat the oil in a frying pan and fry the burgers over a medium heat for 10–15 minutes or until cooked through. Serve with mashed or boiled potatoes and a cold sauce.

Baked courgettes with potatoes

450 g/1 lb courgettes
450 g/1 lb potatoes
100 g/4 oz butter
salt and freshly ground black pepper

Slice the courgettes and place in a colander, sprinkling the layers with a little salt. Cover with a plate and weight it lightly. Leave for 30 minutes, rinse the courgette slices and drain well. Peel and thinly slice the potatoes. Use 25 g/1 oz of the butter to grease an ovenproof dish. Place the courgettes and potatoes in neat layers in the dish, seasoning each layer with salt and pepper and dotting it with butter. Finish with a layer of potatoes and a generous amount of butter. Bake in a moderately hot oven (190 C, 375 F, gas 5) for 45–60 minutes or until well browned.

Forester's sauerkraut

(Illustrated on page 74)

450 g/1 lb canned or bottled sauer-
    kraut
225 g/8 oz smoked pork or cooked
    ham, diced
100 g/4 oz garlic sausage, sliced
50 g/2 oz dripping or butter
1 medium onion, chopped
40 g/1½ oz plain flour
1 teaspoon paprika
salt and freshly ground black pepper

Rinse the sauerkraut and place in a saucepan. Pour over water to cover, bring to the boil and simmer for 30 minutes. Stir in the smoked pork or ham and garlic sausage and heat through thoroughly. Melt the dripping or butter and fry the onion until soft but not browned. Stir in the flour and paprika and cook for 2 minutes. Add this mixture to the sauerkraut and stir well, until the mixture thickens. Season to taste with salt and pepper. Serve with wholewheat bread or boiled potatoes.

Herb pancakes with asparagus

(Illustrated on page 75)

200 g/7 oz plain flour
salt and freshly ground black pepper
2 eggs, separated
300 ml/½ pint milk
2 tablespoons single cream
1 tablespoon chopped chives
1 tablespoon capers, chopped
1–2 teaspoons dried tarragon
75 g/3 oz butter
225 g/8 oz fresh cooked or canned
    asparagus

Sift the flour into a bowl with salt and pepper to taste. Make a well in the centre and add the egg yolks, milk and cream. Mix until smooth. Whisk the egg whites until they form stiff peaks, then fold in with the chives, capers and tarragon. Melt a little of the butter at a time in a small frying pan and pour in batter to cover the base. Cook until set, then flip over and brown the second side. Repeat until all the batter is used up: this should produce six pancakes. Fill the pancakes with asparagus and serve with a salad of your choice.

Forester's sauerkraut

Herb pancakes with asparagus

Courgette omelette

Courgette omelette

(Illustrated on page 75)

4 small courgettes
4 tablespoons oil
6 eggs, separated
salt and freshly ground black pepper
1 tablespoon chopped chives

Clean and slice the courgettes. Heat the oil in a deep frying pan, add the sliced courgettes and fry. Mix the egg yolks with salt and pepper to taste and the finely chopped chives. Whisk the egg whites until they form soft peaks and fold into the yolks. Pour the mixture over the courgettes in the frying pan and cook over a medium heat until set. If desired, the top may be browned by placing the pan briefly under a grill pre-heated to its hottest setting.

Savoy cabbage
with scrambled eggs

450 g/1 lb Savoy cabbage
50 g/2 oz butter
2 tablespoons oil
1 large onion, chopped
6 eggs
salt and freshly ground black pepper
1 teaspoon caraway seeds

Shred the cabbage and cook in boiling salted water for 5–10 minutes or until just soft. Drain well and chop finely. Heat the butter and oil together in a frying pan and fry the onion until just beginning to colour. Add the cabbage and heat through thoroughly. Lightly beat the eggs with salt and pepper to taste and mix in the caraway seeds. Pour the eggs over the hot cabbage and continue cooking until just set. Serve hot with boiled potatoes.

Vegetable soufflé
pancakes

100 g/4 oz plain flour
25 g/1 oz semolina
pinch salt
2 eggs, separated
250 ml/8 fl oz milk
100 g/4 oz cauliflower, broken into florets
75 g /3 oz frozen or fresh peas
1 large carrot, diced
75 g/3 oz cooked ham, diced
1 tablespoon finely chopped chives
4 tablespoons oil

Mix together the flour, semolina and salt in a basin. Make a well in the centre and add the egg yolks and milk. Mix to a smooth batter. Cook the cauliflower, peas and carrot in boiling salted water for a few minutes and drain. Whisk the egg whites until they form soft peaks. Fold the vegetable mixture, ham and chives into the batter, followed by the egg whites. Heat the oil in the frying pan and use the batter to make four pancakes, turning once to brown both sides. Serve as a main dish, accompanied by a fresh green salad.

Savoy cabbage au gratin

1 small Savoy cabbage weighing
    450–675 g/1–1½ lb
100 g/4 oz thinly sliced bacon
40 g/1½ oz butter
4 eggs
150 ml/¼ pint single cream
salt and freshly ground black pepper
1 tablespoon chopped chives
100 g/4 oz cheese, grated

Clean the cabbage and cut into quarters. Remove the hard parts of stalk and cook in boiling salted water for 10 minutes or until tender. Drain well. Wrap each quarter in rashers of bacon. Grease an oven-proof dish with the butter and arrange the cabbage in it. Bake for 15 minutes in a moderate oven (180 C, 350 F, gas 4). Beat together the eggs and cream and season with salt and pepper to taste. Stir in the chives and cheese, pour over the cabbage and bake for a further 15–20 minutes, or until set and golden brown.

Vegetable mixture
in baked potatoes

8 medium potatoes
75 g/3 oz streaky bacon, chopped

1 green pepper, deseeded and
   chopped
2 tomatoes, chopped
1 medium onion, chopped
salt and freshly ground black pepper
1 tablespoon chopped chives
40 g/1½ oz butter

Wash the potatoes and boil for
10 minutes in boiling salted water.
Cut the end off each potato and
scoop out the centre. Mix together
the bacon, pepper, tomato and
onion and season with salt and
pepper. Mix in the chives and use
the mixture to stuff the potatoes.
Dot the tops with butter and place
in an ovenproof dish. Bake for
30 minutes in a hot oven (220 C,
425 F, gas 7). These make a good
accompaniment to grilled meat.

Letcho with lamb

575 g/1¼ lb lean lamb (leg or
   shoulder)
1 large onion, chopped
4 tablespoons oil
salt and freshly ground black pepper
1 teaspoon paprika
1 clove garlic, crushed
3 tablespoons concentrated tomato
purée
150 ml/¼ pint water
1 medium green pepper, deseeded
   and chopped
225 g/8 oz tomatoes, peeled and
   chopped

Cut the lamb into thick strips. Fry
the onion in oil until soft and add

the meat. Turn up the heat and
fry the lamb until browned on all
sides. Add seasoning to taste and
sprinkle over the paprika and garlic.
Stir in the tomato purée and water
and simmer over a low heat for
1 hour. Add the pepper and simmer
for a further 30 minutes. Just before
serving stir in the chopped tomato. Bring back to simmering point
before serving with boiled or baked
potatoes.

Vegetable fondue

(Illustrated on page 78)

1 clove garlic, halved
150 ml/¼ pint white wine
450 g/1 lb Emmental or Cheddar
   cheese, grated
25 g/1 oz cornflour
100 ml/4 fl oz single cream
3 tablespoons kirsch
pinch freshly grated nutmeg
freshly ground black pepper
1 tablespoon chopped chives
50 g/2 oz button mushrooms,
   chopped
vegetables for serving (see method)

Rub the inside of a fondue pan
with the garlic and pour in the
wine. Allow it to heat through. Add
the cheese and stir well. Leave
until melted. Blend the cornflour
with the cream and stir into the
cheese mixture. Add the kirsch,
nutmeg and pepper and stir well.
Just before serving stir in the chives
and mushrooms. Serve with a selection of raw or lightly boiled veg-

etables to dip into the sauce (for
example carrot, celery, leek, cauliflower, sweetcorn), cubes of ham
and slices of crusty French bread.

Stuffed marrow

(Illustrated on page 79)

1 medium vegetable or custard
   marrow
450 g/1 lb pork or veal mince
50 g/2 oz fresh white breadcrumbs
1 onion, finely chopped
2 tablespoons white wine
1 egg, beaten
salt and freshly ground black pepper
pinch freshly grated nutmeg
butter for greasing the dish
Garnish (optional):
   fried tomatoes
   pickles of your choice

Peel the marrow and halve lengthways. Scoop out the seeds with
a spoon. If using a custard marrow
do not peel. Cut off the stalk end
and scoop out the seeds as above.
Mix together the mince, breadcrumbs, onion, wine and egg and
season well with salt, pepper and
nutmeg. Fill the marrow with this
mixture, place in a greased ovenproof dish, cover and cook in
a moderate oven (180 C, 350 F,
gas 4) for 1 hour or until the
marrow is tender. About 15 minutes
before the end of the cooking time
remove the lid to allow the filling
to brown. Garnish with fried tomatoes and various pickles, if desired.

◄ *Vegetable fondue*

Letcho omelette

Stuffed marrow

Mushroom-stuffed cabbage

8 large cabbage leaves
75 g/3 oz butter
1 large onion, chopped
450 g/1 lb mushrooms, chopped
4 eggs, beaten
1–2 tablespoons dry breadcrumbs
salt and freshly ground black pepper
150 ml/¼ pint stock or water

Blanch the cabbage leaves in boiling salted water for 5 minutes. Drain and flatten the broad ribs slightly with the back of a wooden spoon. Melt 50 g/2 oz of the butter and fry the onion until soft. Add the mushrooms and fry until the juice runs. Leave to simmer until most of the juice has evaporated. Pour over the eggs mixed with the breadcrumbs and season well with salt and black pepper. If the mixture is too wet add some more breadcrumbs. Divide the mixture between the cabbage leaves and roll up to make neat parcels. Place in an ovenproof dish, greased with the remaining butter, pour over the stock or water and bake in a moderate oven (180 C, 350 F, gas 4) for 30 minutes. Serve with boiled rice or baked potatoes.

Braised duck with vegetables

4 duck breast portions
75 g/3 oz streaky bacon, chopped
1 large onion, chopped
salt and freshly ground black pepper
1 red or green pepper, chopped
175 g/6 oz small new potatoes, scrubbed
300 ml/½ pint stock or water
1 tablespoon concentrated tomato purée
100 g/4 oz frozen or fresh peas
100 g/4 oz French beans, chopped
1 tablespoon chopped parsley

Bone the duck and cut the meat into strips. Fry the bacon until the fat runs, then add the onion and fry until soft. Add the strips of duck to the pan and fry quickly until browned on all sides. Season well with salt and pepper. Place in an ovenproof dish with the pepper and potatoes. Pour over the stock and tomato purée. Cover and cook in a moderate oven (180 C, 350 F, gas 4) for 1 hour or until the duck is tender. About 15 minutes before the end of the cooking time, stir in the peas and beans. Sprinkle with parsley just before serving with rice and a cucumber salad.

Letcho omelette

(Illustrated on page 79)

3 tablespoons oil
1 large onion, chopped
1 medium green pepper, deseeded and sliced
1 medium red pepper, deseeded and sliced
2 tomatoes, chopped
100 g/4 oz cooked ham, chopped
salt
8 eggs
40 g/1½ oz butter
4 tablespoons tomato chutney or ketchup
40 g/1½ oz blanched almonds
pepper rings to garnish

Heat the oil in a saucepan and fry the onion until soft but not browned. Add the peppers and continue to fry until they begin to soften. Add the tomato, ham and salt to taste and simmer for five minutes. Keep the filling warm while you make the omelettes. Use 2 eggs at a time to make an omelette. Heat a quarter of the butter in a frying pan and beat the eggs lightly with a pinch of salt. When the butter is foaming pour in the eggs and tilt the pan so that the egg covers the base. When cooked to taste put a quarter of the pepper mixture in the centre, fold over the omelette and slide onto a warmed plate. Top each omelette with a spoonful of chutney or ketchup and scatter with almonds. Garnish the plate with rings of pepper.

Puréed carrots

(Illustrated on page 82)

675 g/1½ lb carrots
freshly grated nutmeg
pinch salt
50 g/2 oz butter

Garnish (optional):
    walnut halves, reserved cooked
    carrot slices, lettuce leaves

Scrape and slice the carrots and cook in boiling salted water for 10–15 minutes or until tender. Drain well, then either mash well and sieve or purée in a liquidizer or food processor. Melt the butter in a saucepan and return the purée to the heat. Season to taste with salt and nutmeg. Turn into a serving dish and garnish with walnut halves, slices of carrot and lettuce leaves, if desired.

Cabbage and liver hash

(Illustrated on page 82)

350 g/12 oz Savoy cabbage
100 g/4 oz streaky bacon, chopped
1 medium onion, chopped
1 clove garlic, crushed
225 g/8 oz lamb's or calf's liver, minced
2 eggs, beaten
salt and freshly ground black pepper
1 teaspoon dried marjoram
butter for greasing
Garnish (optional):
    slices ham
    cooked Brussels sprouts

Cook the cabbage in boiling salted water for 10 minutes until soft. Drain well and chop finely. Fry the bacon until the fat runs. Add the onion and garlic and fry until

soft. Stir in the minced liver and continue frying until cooked. Add the cabbage and eggs and season with salt, pepper and marjoram. Turn into a greased tin and bake in a moderately hot oven (200 C, 400 F, gas 6) for 30 minutes. Garnish with slices of ham and halved Brussels sprouts, if desired.

Baked celeriac with cauliflower and ham

(Illustrated on page 82)

225 g/8 oz celeriac, peeled
225 g/8 oz cauliflower florets
75 g/3 oz butter
40 g/1½ oz plain flour
150 ml/¼ pint single cream or creamy milk
salt and freshly ground white pepper
pinch dried mace
4 eggs, beaten
50 g/2 oz fresh white breadcrumbs
225 g/8 oz cooked ham, sliced
parsley sprigs to garnish

Peel the celeriac and cook in boiling salted water for 45 minutes or until soft. Drain and chop coarsely. Cook the cauliflower for 5–10 minutes in boiling water and drain. Melt 50 g/2 oz of the butter in a saucepan and stir in the flour. Cook for 1–2 minutes, then add the cream or milk. Bring to simmering point and season to taste with salt, pepper and mace. Stir in the eggs, bread-crumbs and celeriac. Grease an ovenproof dish with the remaining

butter and fill with the celeriac mixture. Bake in a moderate oven (160 C, 325 F, gas 3) for 30 minutes. Arrange the slices of ham and cauliflower florets on top of the mixture and return to the oven for a further 15 minutes or until just beginning to brown. Garnish with sprigs of parsley.

Caramelized cabbage

450 g/1 lb red cabbage
75 g/3 oz sugar
salt
1 teaspoon caraway seeds
2 tablespoons vinegar or white wine
1 large onion, chopped
25 g/1 oz dripping or white vegetable fat
15 g/½ oz plain flour

Remove any stalk from the cabbage and shred the leaves. Blanch in boiling salted water for 3 minutes and drain well. Heat the sugar in a saucepan until it caramelizes. Add the cabbage, salt to taste, caraway seeds and a dash of vinegar or white wine and braise for 5 minutes. Fry the onion in the dripping until soft, then stir in the flour to make a smooth paste. Add this mixture to the cabbage, cook gently for a few more minutes and serve. The cabbage must not be too soft. This goes well with roast pork and smoked meat.

German Easter stuffing

Baked celeriac with cauliflower and ham, Cabbage and liver hash, Puréed carrots

Japanese vegetable tempura ▶

Vegetable pizza

½ teaspoon sugar
150 ml/¼ pint lukewarm water
15 g/½ oz dried yeast
250 g/9 oz plain flour
pinch salt
2 tablespoons oil
4 tablespoons concentrated tomato
    purée
½ teaspoon oregano
2 cloves garlic, crushed
2 large tomatoes, sliced
1 medium green pepper, deseeded
    and chopped
100 g/4 oz mushrooms, sliced
1 large onion, sliced into rings
100 g/4 oz Cheddar cheese, grated

Dissolve the sugar in the water and sprinkle over the yeast. Leave for 10 minutes in a warm place, until frothy. Sift the flour into a large bowl with the salt and make a well in the centre. Pour in the yeast mixture and mix to a smooth dough. Knead the dough until smooth and elastic. Place inside an oiled plastic bag and leave until doubled in size.

Mix together the oil, tomato purée, oregano and garlic. Turn the risen dough onto a floured board and knead for a few minutes. Divide into four portions, roll these into a ball and press into flat rounds on an oiled baking sheet. Spread with the tomato mixture and leave in a warm place for 15 minutes. Top with slices of tomato, pepper, mushroom and onion and bake in a hot oven (220 C, 425 F, gas 7)

for 20 minutes. Sprinkle over the cheese and return to the oven for a further 10 minutes or until the cheese is golden and bubbling.

German Easter stuffing

(Illustrated on page 82)

4 (1-cm/½-in thick) slices stale white
    bread
100 ml/4 fl oz single cream
75 g/3 oz butter
4 eggs, separated
225 g/8 oz smoked pork or cooked
    ham, diced
salt and freshly ground black pepper
pinch dried mace
12 tablespoons dry breadcrumbs
100 g/4 oz young nettle leaves or
    cooked spinach, finely chopped

Remove the crusts from the bread and dice. Pour over the cream and leave to soak for a few minutes. Cream 50 g/2 oz of the butter with the egg yolks and mix with the softened bread and meat. Season well with salt, pepper and mace. Grease a flameproof dish or loaf tin with the remaining butter and sprinkle with the breadcrumbs. Beat the egg whites with a pinch of salt until they form soft peaks and fold in the nettle leaves or spinach. Fold the egg whites into the stuffing, turn into the prepared dish and cook in a moderate oven (160 C, 325 F, gas 3) for 1–1¼ hours or until golden brown. Serve with a crisp green salad as an accompa-

niment to cold roast chicken or turkey.

Japanese vegetable tempura

(Illustrated on page 83)

1 large carrot
1 large leek
2 sticks celery
100 g/4 oz mushrooms
2 eggs
pinch salt
450 ml/¾ pint water
200 g/7 oz plain flour
oil for frying
soy sauce for serving

Cut the carrot, leek and celery into strips and slice the mushrooms. Make a thin batter out of the eggs, salt, cold water and flour. Fold in the vegetables and stir lightly. Heat the oil in a frying pan. Drop in spoonfuls of the vegetable batter and fry until golden brown on both sides. Serve with soy sauce handed separately.

Cabbage rolls with vegetable stuffing

4 large cabbage leaves
100 g/4 oz carrots
40 g/1½ oz butter
100 g/4 oz cauliflower florets

100 g/4 oz French beans, chopped
salt and freshly ground black pepper
150 ml/$\frac{1}{4}$ pint stock or water
100 g/4 oz frozen or fresh peas
2 eggs, beaten
75 g/3 oz streaky bacon, chopped
1 medium onion, chopped

Blanch the cabbage leaves in boiling water for 5 minutes. Drain well. Dice the carrots and fry in the butter for 5 minutes. Add the cauliflower, French beans, salt, pepper and a little of the stock or water. Cover the pan closely and simmer for 10–15 minutes or until the vegetables are tender. Add the peas and return to the boil. Drain off surplus liquid and pour over the beaten eggs. Stir gently over the heat until the eggs set. Pile spoonfuls of the mixture on the blanched cabbage leaves and roll into neat parcels. Fry the bacon until the fat runs, add the onion and fry until soft. Spread this mixture over the base of an ovenproof dish and place the cabbage parcels on top. Pour over the remaining stock or water, cover and cook in a moderate oven (180 C, 350 F, gas 4) for 30 minutes.

Baked cabbage with pasta

450 g/1 lb cabbage, shredded
75 g/3 oz streaky bacon, chopped
1 large onion, chopped
salt and freshly ground black pepper
225 g/8 oz pasta shapes
butter for greasing
2 eggs
150 ml/$\frac{1}{4}$ pint single cream
pinch ground mace
1 tablespoon chopped parsley

Blanch the cabbage in boiling water for 3 minutes. Drain well. Fry the bacon until the fat runs and add the onion. Fry until soft. Add the cabbage with a good seasoning of salt and pepper and continue cooking until the cabbage is just soft. Cook the pasta in boiling salted water according to the directions on the packet. Drain well and mix with the cabbage. Grease an ovenproof dish with butter and turn the cabbage mixture into it. Beat the eggs with the cream and season with salt, pepper and mace. Stir in the parsley and pour the mixture over the pasta. Bake in a moderate oven (160 C, 325 F, gas 3) for 30–40 minutes until golden brown.

Baked vegetable ham rolls

(Illustrated on page 86)

100 g/4 oz cauliflower florets
100 g/4 oz red pepper, deseeded and chopped
100 g/4 oz broccoli
50 g/2 oz butter
1 egg
salt and freshly ground white pepper
4 (25-g/1-oz) slices of ham
4 egg yolks
4 tablespoons double cream
75 g/3 oz cheese, grated
1 tablespoon chopped parsley

Cook the vegetables in boiling salted water until just soft. Drain and put in a saucepan with 40 g/1$\frac{1}{2}$ oz butter. Stir over a low heat until coated. Add the egg and season to taste with salt and pepper. Spoon the mixture on the ham slices and roll them up. Grease an ovenproof dish with the remaining butter and transfer the rolls into the dish. Pour over the egg yolks mixed with the cream and grated cheese and bake in a moderate oven (180 C, 350 F, gas 4) for 15–20 minutes or until the top is golden brown. Serve with a crisp green salad.

Variation:
Fried vegetable ham rolls

(Illustrated on page 87)

Use 100 g/4 oz carrots, peas and kohlrabi instead of the cauliflower, peppers and broccoli. Instead of baking the rolls in eggs and cream roll them in flour, then dip in egg and breadcrumbs and deep fry until golden brown. Serve with a green salad and wedges of lemon.

Baked vegetable ham rolls ▶
Fried vegetable rolls

Cabbage
and ham pancakes

2 eggs, separated
salt and freshly ground black pepper
250 ml/8 fl oz milk
175 g/6 oz plain flour
100 g/4 oz cooked ham, chopped
225 g/8 oz cabbage, finely shredded
4 tablespoons oil

Combine the egg yolks, salt, pepper, milk and flour to make the batter. Stir in the chopped ham and cabbage. Whisk the egg whites until they form soft peaks and fold into the batter. Heat the oil in a large frying pan and pour in the batter. Fry until browned underneath and set. Turn carefully and brown the other side. Serve warm, cut into wedges.

Carrot pancakes

2 medium carrots
50 g/2 oz butter
75 g/3 oz plain flour
150 ml/$\frac{1}{4}$ pint milk
salt and freshly ground white pepper
2 eggs, beaten
100 g/4 oz cooked ham, chopped
2 tablespoons oil

Dice the carrots very finely and blanch in boiling salted water for 5 minutes, then drain. Melt the butter, stir in the flour and cook for 1–2 minutes. Add the milk and

salt and pepper to taste and bring to the boil, stirring all the time. Remove from the heat and add the eggs, ham and carrots. Mix together well. Heat the oil in the pan and drop in spoonfuls of the mixture. Fry until brown on both sides. Serve with mashed potatoes and a crisp green salad.

Creamed celeriac
with fish

450 g/1 lb celeriac
1 large onion, chopped
75 g/3 oz butter
2 teaspoons lemon juice
salt and freshly ground black pepper
675 g/1$\frac{1}{2}$ lb white fish (e.g. haddock, cod, coley)
300 ml/$\frac{1}{4}$ pint vegetable stock or water
25 g/1 oz plain flour
100 ml/4 fl oz single cream
dill sprigs to garnish (optional)

Cut the celeriac into strips and fry together with the chopped onion in the butter. When the vegetables begin to soften, add the lemon juice and salt and pepper to taste. Lay the fish on top of the celeriac and add enough of the stock to cover the vegetables. Simmer gently for 15–20 minutes, until the fish is cooked and firm. Remove the fish from the pan and lay on a warmed serving dish. Keep warm. Sprinkle the flour into the pan and add the cream. Heat gently until simmering

point is reached. Remove from the heat at once and pour the creamed celeriac over the fish. Garnish with sprigs of dill, if using.

Mushroom-stuffed
celeriac

2 medium celeriacs
2 small onions, chopped
40 g/1$\frac{1}{2}$ oz butter
100 g/4 oz mushrooms, chopped
salt and freshly ground white pepper
2 eggs, beaten
8 rashers streaky bacon

Peel the celeriacs and slice each one into four thick slices. Cook in boiling salted water for 15–20 minutes or until soft. Fry the onion in butter, add the mushrooms, salt and pepper and cook until all the liquid has evaporated. Stir in the eggs and cook until the mixture thickens. Spread the stuffing on four of the celeriac slices and cover with the remaining four slices. Wrap the celeriac 'sandwiches' in the rashers of bacon and place in an ovenproof dish. Bake in a moderately hot oven (190 C, 375 F, gas 5) for 20–30 minutes or until the bacon is cooked and crisp.

Variation:
Ham-stuffed celeriac

Omit the mushroom stuffing and sandwich the celeriac together with slices of ham. Drip in batter as for Deep-fried carrots (page 92) and deep fry until golden.

Salami-stuffed celeriac

Use salami to sandwich together the prepared celeriac. Coat in egg and breadcrumbs and shallow fry until golden brown on both sides.

Vegetables in mustard sauce

100 g/4 oz carrots
100 g/4 oz kohlrabi
100 g/4 oz French beans
100 g/4 oz frozen or fresh peas
75 g/3 oz butter
1 small onion, chopped
40 g/1$\frac{1}{2}$ oz plain flour
100 ml/4 fl oz milk
100 ml/4 fl oz double cream
1 teaspoon dried tarragon
salt and freshly ground white pepper
2 tablespoons prepared mustard

Cook the carrots, kohlrabi, French beans and peas in boiling salted water until just tender. Drain, reserving the stock, and keep warm. Melt the butter in a saucepan and fry the onion until soft but not browned. Stir in the flour and cook for 2 minutes. Add the milk and bring to the boil, stirring all the time. Add the cream and tarragon and season to taste with salt and pepper. Stir in the mustard and

a little of the reserved vegetable stock if the sauce is too thick. Strain over the cooked vegetables and serve as an accompaniment to boiled or roast beef.

Vegetable goulash

(Illustrated on page 90)

2 tablespoons oil
1 large onion, chopped
1–2 teaspoons paprika
2 cloves garlic, crushed
2 medium carrots, chopped
2 sticks celery, chopped
1 small cauliflower, broken into florets
1 red or green pepper, deseeded and chopped
10 cocktail onions
600 ml/1 pint vegetable stock
2 tablespoons concentrated tomato purée
salt
4 medium tomatoes, chopped
25 g/1 oz butter
25 g/1 oz plain flour
150 ml/$\frac{1}{4}$ pint soured cream
1 tablespoon chopped chives

Heat the oil in a large saucepan and fry the onion until soft but not brown. Stir in the paprika and garlic and fry for a further 2 minutes. Add the carrot, celery, cauliflower, pepper and cocktail onions and pour over the stock and tomato purée. Season to taste with salt and simmer for 15 minutes or until the vegetables are just soft.

Stir in the tomatoes. Knead the butter with the flour and drop small pieces of the mixture into the goulash, stirring until the sauce thickens. Finally turn into a warmed serving dish and swirl in the soured cream and sprinkle with chopped chives. Serve with pasta shapes or noodles.

Carrots with almonds and horseradish

450 g/1 lb carrots
300 ml/$\frac{1}{2}$ pint beef stock
50 g/2 oz butter
25 g/1 oz plain flour
salt and freshly ground white pepper
2 egg yolks
100 ml/4 fl oz double cream
25 g/1 oz horseradish, grated
50 g/2 oz blanched almonds, chopped

Cut the carrots into strips and simmer in the beef stock until just soft. Drain, reserving the stock. Melt the butter in a saucepan and stir in the flour. Cook gently for 1–2 minutes. Add the stock, salt and pepper to taste and bring to the boil, stirring all the time. Mix the egg yolks with the cream and stir into the sauce. Remove from the heat and stir in the horseradish and almonds. Finally fold in the carrots. Serve with boiled beef or roast pork.

Vegetable goulash

Stuffed lettuce au gratin

Stuffed cauliflower ▶

Stuffed lettuce au gratin

(*Illustrated on page 90*)

4 heads lettuce, halved
75 g/3 oz cooked ham, chopped
75 g/3 oz butter
2 eggs, beaten
salt and freshly ground black pepper
4 tomatoes, quartered
2 egg yolks
3 tablespoons double cream
50 g/2 oz Emmental cheese, grated

Blanch the lettuce briefly in boiling salted water, drain and spread the leaves on a wooden board. Fry the ham in 50 g/2 oz of the butter, stir in the eggs and salt and pepper to taste and cook until set. Divide the mixture between the lettuce leaves, roll them up and arrange in a greased ovenproof dish with the tomatoes and dot with the remaining butter. Place in a moderately hot oven (190 C, 375 F, gas 5) for a few minutes. Pour over the egg yolks beaten with the cream, seasoning and grated cheese. Return to the oven and bake for 20–25 minutes or until golden brown.

Stuffed cauliflower

(*Illustrated on page 91*)

450 g/1 lb pork or beef mince
a little oil for frying
100 g/4 oz cooked ham or salami, finely chopped
1 medium onion, finely chopped

75 g/3 oz fresh white breadcrumbs
1 egg, beaten
salt and freshly ground black pepper
1 large cauliflower
butter for greasing
75 g/3 oz Emmental cheese, grated
Garnish:
   bunch spring onions, chopped
   tomato wedges

First fry the mince for 10 minutes in a little oil until it has browned all over. Then mix together the mince, ham or salami, onion and breadcrumbs. Add the beaten egg and season to taste with salt and pepper. Cook the whole cauliflower in boiling salted water for about 15 minutes or until just beginning to soften. Drain and place upside-down in a deep bowl and scoop out the core. Fill with the meat mixture and turn the right way up in a greased, shallow ovenproof dish. Sprinkle with the grated cheese and bake in a moderate oven (180 C, 350 F, gas 4) for 45–60 minutes or until golden. Garnish with chopped spring onions and wedges of tomato.

Deep-fried carrots

8 medium carrots
100 g/4 oz plain flour
salt
1 egg
150 ml/¼ pint milk
oil for frying

Cut the carrots lengthways into quarters and cook in boiling salted water until just tender. Drain well. Sift the flour and a pinch of salt into a basin and make a well in the centre. Add the egg and half the milk and mix until smooth. Add the rest of the milk. Heat the oil in a deep-frier and coat the carrots with batter. Deep fry in small batches until golden.

Spinach cannelloni

(*Illustrated on page 94*)

200 g/7 oz plain flour
salt and freshly ground black pepper
4 eggs
75 g/3 oz cooked spinach, very finely chopped
1 large onion, chopped
75 g/3 oz butter
100 g/4 oz mushrooms, chopped
100 g/4 oz chicken liver, chopped
100 g/4 oz ham, chopped
1 teaspoon oregano
100 g/4 oz Cheddar cheese, grated
Garnish:
   black olives
   tomato slices

Sift the flour with a pinch of salt into a bowl and break in two of the eggs. Add the spinach and mix to a smooth dough, adding a little extra flour if it is too moist. Roll out very thinly or feed through the rollers of a pasta machine. Cut into 12-cm/5-in squares. Cook in boiling salted water for a few minutes until just tender. Drain and spread out to dry. Fry the onion in 50 g/2 oz of the butter until soft, add the mushrooms and chicken liver and fry until cooked through. Stir in the ham, pour over the remaining two beaten eggs, add salt, pepper and oregano and cook until the eggs are set. Fill the squares with this mixture and roll them up. Grease an ovenproof dish with the remaining butter and put the cannelloni in the dish. Top with the grated cheese and bake in a moderately hot oven (200 C, 400 F, gas 6) for 20–25 minutes or until golden and bubbling. Garnish with slices of tomato and black olives.

Braised aubergine with tongue

(Illustrated on page 94)

50 g/2 oz butter
1 medium onion, chopped
2 medium aubergines, diced
salt and freshly ground black pepper
1 tablespoon concentrated tomato purée
100 g/4 oz tomatoes, chopped
1 tablespoon chopped chives
350 g/12 oz cooked tongue, sliced
Garnish:
    strips of celery
    tomato slices

Melt the butter and fry the onion until soft but not browned. Add the aubergine, salt and pepper to taste and the tomato purée. Cover and cook over a low heat until the aubergine is tender. Stir in the tomato and chives and heat through. Serve topped with slices of tongue and garnished with pieces of celery and slices of tomato. Serve with fried potatoes or crusty French bread.

Ham-stuffed aubergine

(Illustrated on page 95)

2 medium aubergines
75 g/3 oz butter
3 tablespoons single cream
2 slices white bread, crusts removed and diced
75 g/3 oz ham, chopped
2 eggs, beaten
1 tablespoon chopped parsley
salt and freshly ground white pepper
pinch freshly grated nutmeg
75 g/3 oz Cheddar cheese, grated

Halve the aubergines, scoop out the flesh and chop it. Melt 50 g/2 oz of the butter and cook the aubergine flesh until tender. Blanch the shells in boiling water for 5 minutes. Pour the cream over the bread and add this to the cooked aubergine flesh with the ham, eggs, parsley and salt, pepper and nutmeg to taste. Fill the aubergine shells with the mixture, sprinkle with the cheese and sandwich together to re-form the original shape. Dot with the remaining butter and place in an ovenproof dish. Bake in a moderately hot oven (200 C, 400 F, gas 6) for 30 minutes.

Stuffed cucumber

(Illustrated on page 95)

450 g/1 lb beef or pork mince
50 g/2 oz fresh breadcrumbs
1 small onion, finely chopped
1 egg, beaten
salt and freshly ground black pepper
pinch freshly grated nutmeg
1 teaspoon grated lemon rind
1 large cucumber
2 tablespoons tomato chutney or ketchup to garnish

Mix together the mince, breadcrumbs, onion and egg. Season with salt, pepper, nutmeg and lemon rind. Peel the cucumber and halve lengthways. Scoop out the seeds and fill with the meat mixture. Re-form the cucumber shape and tie up with string (see page 27). Wrap in aluminium foil and place on a baking sheet. Cook in a moderately hot oven (200 C, 400 F, gas 6) for 30–35 minutes or until the filling is cooked. Remove carefully from the foil and slice the cucumber. Garnish with small spoonfuls of tomato chutney or ketchup. Serve with rice and a crisp green salad.

Spinach cannelloni

Braised aubergine with tongue

Ham-stuffed aubergine ▶

Stuffed cucumber ▶

Mixed vegetables with bacon

150 g/5 oz streaky bacon, chopped
1 large onion, chopped
1 clove garlic, crushed
450 g/1 lb cooked mixed vegetables
    (e.g. carrots, French beans,
    Brussels sprouts)
salt and freshly ground black pepper
1 tablespoon chopped chives

Fry the bacon until the fat runs. Add the onion and garlic and fry until soft. Dice the vegetables and add to the pan. Fry over a medium heat, stirring from time to time until heated through. Season well with salt and pepper and stir in the chives. This goes well with roast meat.

Baked soufflé vegetables

100 g/4 oz butter
100 g/4 oz plain flour
250 ml/8 fl oz single cream
4 eggs, separated
pinch ground mace
1 tablespoon chopped chives
salt and freshly ground black pepper
50 g/2 oz fresh white breadcrumbs
100 g/4 oz cooked mixed vegetables
    (e.g. cauliflower florets, diced
    carrots, peas, chopped asparagus)

Melt all but 15 g/$\frac{1}{2}$ oz of the butter, then stir in the flour and cook gently for 1–2 minutes. Add the cream and bring just to the boil. Cool slightly and stir in the egg yolks, mace, chives and salt and pepper to taste. Add the bread-crumbs and mix well. Whisk the egg whites until stiff. Fold the vegetables into the cream sauce followed by the egg whites. Turn into a soufflé dish, greased with the remaining butter and bake in a moderate oven (180 C, 350 F, gas 4) for 30–35 minutes until risen and golden brown. Serve with a mixed salad.

Mixed vegetable rolls

100 g/4 oz carrots, diced
100 g/4 oz cauliflower florets
1 stick celery, chopped
100 g/4 oz frozen or fresh peas
50 g/2 oz butter
1 tablespoon chopped chives
salt and freshly ground black pepper
4 eggs, beaten
8 slices smoked pork or cooked
    ham

Cook the carrots, cauliflower and celery in boiling salted water for a few minutes until they are just beginning to soften. Add the peas and return to the boil. Remove from the heat and drain. Melt 40 g/1$\frac{1}{2}$ oz of the butter, add the chives and drained vegetables and season to taste with salt and pepper. Stir in the eggs and cook until they are set. Spread the pork or ham slices with this mixture, roll them up and arrange in an ovenproof dish. Dot with the remaining butter and bake in a moderately hot oven (200 C, 400 F, gas 6) for 15–20 minutes. Serve with mashed potatoes or any potato accompaniment and a crisp green salad.

Baked lettuce with ham

4 heads lettuce
butter for greasing
100 g/4 oz cooked ham, diced
4 eggs, beaten
salt and freshly ground black pepper
75 g/3 oz Cheddar cheese, grated

Shred the lettuce coarsely and blanch for 1–2 minutes in boiling salted water. Drain well. Grease an ovenproof dish with butter, arrange the lettuce in the dish and place the diced ham in the middle. Lightly beat the eggs and season to taste. Combine with the grated cheese and pour over the ham and lettuce. Bake in a moderate oven (180 C, 350 F, gas 4) for 25–30 minutes. Serve with boiled potatoes or crusty bread rolls.

Creamy baked lettuce

2 heads lettuce
butter for greasing
4 tablespoons double cream
4 egg yolks
100 g/4 oz Emmental cheese, grated

salt and freshly ground white pepper
pinch freshly grated nutmeg

Halve the lettuces. Blanch in boiling salted water for 2 minutes. Drain well. Grease four individual gratin dishes with butter and arrange the lettuce in them. Mix together the cream, egg yolks and grated cheese and season well with salt, pepper and nutmeg. Pour this mixture over the lettuce halves and bake in a moderately hot oven (190 C, 375 F, gas 5) for 20 minutes or until golden brown.

Vegetable spaghetti

40 g/1½ oz butter
1 large onion, chopped
2 cloves garlic, crushed
1 small red or green pepper, chopped
100 g/4 oz mushrooms, sliced
100 g/4 oz frozen or fresh peas
2 large tomatoes, chopped
small bunch radishes (optional)
2 tablespoons concentrated tomato purée
salt and freshly ground black pepper
225 g/8 oz spaghetti
50 g/2 oz Parmesan cheese, finely grated
tomato wedges to garnish

Melt the butter in a saucepan and fry the onion and garlic until soft but not browned. Add the pepper, mushrooms, peas, tomatoes, radishes (if using) and tomato purée.

Season to taste with salt and pepper, cover closely and simmer for 15–20 minutes until the vegetables are tender. Meanwhile cook the spaghetti according to the instructions on the packet. Drain the spaghetti and place in a serving bowl. Top with the vegetable sauce and sprinkle over the cheese. Serve at once garnished with wedges of tomato.

Cauliflower and spaghetti au gratin

1 small cauliflower
225 g/8 oz spaghetti
40 g/1½ oz butter
salt
100 g/4 oz frozen or fresh peas
100 g/4 oz mushrooms, chopped
100 g/4 oz Cheddar cheese, grated

Cook the cauliflower and the spaghetti separately in salted water until just tender. Drain and chop the cauliflower roughly. Drain the spaghetti and place half of it in a large ovenproof dish, greased with a little of the butter. Cover with the cauliflower, a layer of the peas and a layer of the mushrooms. Top with half the grated cheese and cover with the rest of the spaghetti. Sprinkle with the remaining cheese. Melt the remaining butter and drizzle over the spaghetti. Bake in a moderately hot oven (200 C, 400 F, gas 6) for 20–25 minutes or until golden and bubbling.

Chicken with vegetable stuffing

(Illustrated on page 98)

75 g/3 oz butter
50 g/2 oz carrots, finely diced
50 g/2 oz peppers, finely chopped
50 g/2 oz frozen or fresh peas
50 g/2 oz button mushrooms, chopped
salt and freshly ground black pepper
4 eggs
4 chicken quarters (breast and wing)

Melt 50 g/2 oz of the butter and cook the carrots, peppers, peas and mushrooms until just tender. Season to taste with salt and pepper. Stir in the eggs and cook until set. Cut a deep slit in each chicken portion parallel to the bone. Divide the vegetable mixture between the chicken portions, stuffing it well into the 'pocket'. Place them in a roasting tin and dot the remaining butter over them. Cook in a moderate oven (180 C, 350 F, gas 4) for 1 hour. Serve with a mixed salad and potato croquettes.

Asparagus with hollandaise sauce

Chicken with vegetable stuffing

Brussels sprouts with soy sauce ▶

Asparagus with hollandaise sauce

(*Illustrated on page 98*)

450 g/1 lb asparagus spears
salt
1 quantity hollandaise sauce (see
  page 153)
Garnish:
  parsley sprigs
  1 tomato, sliced

Trim the asparagus and cook in boiling salted water or steam until tender. Pour over the hollandaise sauce and garnish with sprigs of parsley and slices of tomato.

Brussels sprouts with soy sauce

(*Illustrated on page 99*)

450 g/1 lb Brussels sprouts
salt and freshly ground black pepper
50 g/2 oz dripping or white
  vegetable fat
100 g/4 oz leeks, sliced
3 cloves garlic, crushed
3 tablespoons soy sauce
1 tablespoon cornflour

Blanch the Brussels sprouts for 5 minutes in boiling salted water. Drain well. Melt the dripping or vegetable fat in a large frying pan and fry the leeks and garlic until soft. Add the Brussels sprouts and fry gently for a further 5 minutes.

Add a good seasoning of pepper, the soy sauce and the cornflour mixed to a smooth paste with a little water. Cook for a further few minutes, turning the sprouts gently in the sauce. Serve as an accompaniment to meat dishes.

Cauliflower with ham

1 large cauliflower
225 g/8 oz cooked ham, chopped
2 tablespoons chopped parsley
4 eggs
100 ml/4 fl oz double cream
salt and freshly ground black pepper
100 g/4 oz Emmental cheese, grated

Wash the cauliflower, break into florets and cook in boiling salted water until soft. Drain and place half the cauliflower in a greased ovenproof dish. Cover with the ham and sprinkle over the parsley. Top with the remaining cauliflower. Beat the eggs with the cream and season well with salt and pepper. Mix in the grated cheese and pour over the cauliflower. Bake in a moderate oven (170 C, 325 F, gas 3) for 30–40 minutes until golden brown.

Aubergine au gratin

40 g/1½ oz butter
1 medium onion, chopped
40 g/1½ oz plain flour
salt and freshly ground black pepper
pinch freshly grated nutmeg
3 tablespoons milk
100 ml/4 fl oz double cream
2 medium aubergines
2 tablespoons oil
4 egg yolks
40 g/1½ oz Parmesan cheese, grated
40 g/1½ oz Emmental cheese, grated

Melt the butter and fry the onion until soft. Stir in the flour to make a smooth paste. Add salt, pepper and nutmeg to taste and then the milk and cream. Bring to the boil, simmer for a couple of minutes and cool. Halve the aubergines and scoop out the flesh. Cut the flesh into small pieces and cook gently in the oil until soft. Stir the egg yolks, aubergine and grated cheeses into the cooled sauce and mix well. Stuff the aubergine shells with the mixture and bake in a moderately hot oven (190 C, 375 F, gas 5) for 30 minutes or until the aubergine shells are soft and the filling golden brown.

Spinach soufflé with ham

(*Illustrated on page 102*)

350 g/12 oz spinach
40 g/1½ oz butter
40 g/1½ oz plain flour
300 ml/½ pint milk
salt and freshly ground black pepper
pinch freshly grated nutmeg
4 eggs, separated
175 g/6 oz cooked ham, chopped

Wash the spinach well and cook in the water clinging to the leaves until tender. Drain well and chop the leaves finely. Melt the butter and stir in the flour. Cook over a low heat for 1–2 minutes. Stir in the milk and bring to the boil, stirring all the time. Season well with salt, pepper and nutmeg. Remove from the heat and beat in the egg yolks. Whisk the egg whites until stiff. Fold the spinach and ham into the sauce, followed by the egg whites. Turn into a greased soufflé dish and bake in a moderate oven (180 C, 350 F, gas 4) until well risen and golden. This goes well with a ham salad.

Variation:

Spinach and cheese soufflé

Omit the ham and add 100 g/4 oz finely grated Cheddar cheese to the sauce with the egg yolks.

Asparagus meunière

(Illustrated on page 102)

450 g/1 lb asparagus
salt and freshly ground white pepper
juice of $\frac{1}{2}$ lemon
50 g/2 oz toasted breadcrumbs
75 g/3 oz butter, melted
Garnish:
    salad vegetables, e.g. tomato, radish, spring onion

Wash and trim the asparagus. Cook in boiling water or steam until just tender. Drain and arrange on warmed serving plates. Season to taste with salt, pepper and lemon juice. Sprinkle over the breadcrumbs and garnish with salad vegetables of your choice. Hand the melted butter separately.

Spinach with cheese

450 g/1 lb spinach
2 small onions, chopped
50 g/2 oz butter
salt and freshly ground black pepper
225 g/8 oz Cheddar cheese, grated
2 eggs, beaten

Wash the spinach and cook in the water clinging to the leaves until tender. Drain well and chop coarsely. Fry the onion in the butter until soft, add the spinach with salt and pepper to taste and stir over a low heat until well mixed. Stir in the grated cheese and eggs and cook for 2 minutes. This makes an excellent filling for omelettes, pancakes, etc.

Chicken with vegetables and dill

50 g/2 oz butter
1 large leek, sliced
2 carrots, chopped
2 sticks celery, chopped

4 boned chicken breasts
salt and freshly ground white pepper
150 ml/$\frac{1}{4}$ pint chicken stock
1 bay leaf
25 g/1 oz plain flour
2 egg yolks
25 g/1 oz dill or parsley
100 ml/4 fl oz double cream

Melt 25 g/1 oz of the butter and fry the leek until soft. Add the carrots and celery and continue frying for a few minutes. Cut the chicken into 1-cm/$\frac{1}{2}$-in strips and add to the pan. Season with salt and pepper to taste. Pour over the stock, add the bay leaf and simmer gently for 25–30 minutes until the chicken is tender. Knead the remaining butter with the flour and add, a little at a time, to the sauce. Blend the egg yolks and finely chopped dill or parsley with the cream, stir into the stew, bring to the boil and remove from the heat. Serve with rice and a lightly cooked green vegetable.

Variation:

Chicken with spring vegetables

Omit the leek and celery and use 100 g/4 oz fresh peas and 100 g/4 oz cauliflower or kohlrabi instead. Omit the dill or parsley and use 1 teaspoon dried or 2 teaspoons fresh chopped tarragon.

Spinach soufflé with ham

Asparagus meunière

Cauliflower with chicken drumsticks

Cauliflower with chicken drumsticks

(Illustrated on page 103)

75 g/3 oz butter
1 large onion, chopped
4 chicken drumsticks
1 large cauliflower
50 g/2 oz plain flour
150 ml/¼ pint chicken stock
salt and freshly ground white pepper
pinch freshly grated nutmeg
2 egg yolks
3 tablespoons double cream
1 tablespoon chopped chives to
     garnish

Melt half the butter in a frying pan and fry the onion until soft. Add the chicken drumsticks and fry until cooked through and tender. While the chicken is cooking divide the cauliflower into florets and cook in boiling salted water until tender. Drain and arrange the cauliflower and chicken drumsticks in a warmed serving dish, keep warm. Add the remaining butter to the pan in which the chicken was cooked and stir in the flour. Cook for 1–2 minutes, then add the chicken stock. Bring to the boil and simmer for 1–2 minutes. Season well with salt, pepper and nutmeg. Remove from the heat and stir in the egg yolks and cream. If the sauce is too thick, add a little of the cauliflower cooking water. Pass the sauce through a sieve over the chicken and cauliflower. Sprinkle over the chives and serve with a rice salad.

Variations:
Cauliflower with ham

Omit the chicken and add 225 g/8 oz diced cooked ham to the sauce. Use ½ teaspoon mustard powder in place of the nutmeg.

Cauliflower with lamb

Omit the chicken and add 225 g/8 oz chopped, left-over roast lamb to the sauce. Use a pinch of dried thyme in place of the nutmeg.

Roman spinach

675 g/1½ lb spinach
50 g/2 oz streaky bacon, chopped
50 g/2 oz butter
25 g/1 oz raisins
salt and freshly ground black pepper
25 g/1 oz pine nuts

Blanch the spinach in boiling salted water for 2 minutes. Drain and cut into strips. Fry the bacon until the fat runs and add the butter, spinach, raisins and salt and pepper to taste. Cook for a few minutes, turning the spinach gently. Turn into a serving dish and sprinkle over the pine nuts.

Variation:
Spinach with bacon

Increase the quantity of bacon to 100 g/4 oz and fry a small finely chopped onion in the fat before adding the spinach. Omit the pine nuts and raisins.

Pork chops with vegetable stuffing

4 pork chops
50 g/2 oz streaky bacon, chopped
1 medium carrot, diced
½ green pepper, chopped
1 leek, sliced
1 stick celery, chopped
25 g/1 oz plain flour
salt and freshly ground black pepper
50 g/2 oz dripping or lard

Cut a pocket in the chops for the stuffing. Fry the bacon until the fat runs and fry the carrot, pepper, leek and celery until soft. Use the vegetable mixture to stuff the chops. Close each pocket with a wooden cocktail stick. Dip each chop in seasoned flour and fry in the dripping or lard for 20–25 minutes, turning once, until golden and cooked through. Remove the cocktail sticks before serving.

Beetroot pudding

225 g/8 oz beetroot
50 g/2 oz butter
50 g/2 oz plain flour
100 ml/4 fl oz chicken stock
100 ml/4 fl oz double cream
4 eggs, separated
25 g/1 oz fresh white breadcrumbs

salt and freshly ground black pepper
pinch ground mace

Cook the whole unpeeled beetroot in boiling salted water for about 40 minutes until tender. Drain and peel the beetroot, chop roughly and press through a sieve. Melt the butter and stir in the flour. Add the stock and bring to the boil. Simmer for 2 minutes. Remove from the heat and add the cream, egg yolks, breadcrumbs and beetroot. Season to taste with salt, pepper and mace. Whisk the egg whites until stiff and fold into the sauce. Turn the mixture into a greased soufflé dish. Simmer slowly in a bain-marie for 25–30 minutes. This goes well with poultry or veal.

Baked eggs with spinach

(Illustrated on page 106)

225 g/8 oz spinach
25 g/1 oz butter
4 eggs
2 egg yolks
2 tablespoons double cream
75 g/3 oz Cheddar cheese, grated
salt and freshly ground black pepper

Boil the spinach in salted water until tender. Drain well. Grease four flameproof ramekins with the butter and line with spinach leaves. Poach the eggs and place one in each ramekin. Pour over a mixture of the egg yolks, cream and grated cheese, seasoned with salt and pepper. Place

under a pre-heated grill until golden brown. Serve with a mixed salad.

Deep-fried peppers

(Illustrated on page 106)

675 g/1½ lb green peppers
salt
25 g/1 oz plain flour
1 egg, beaten
25 g/1 oz dry breadcrumbs
oil for deep frying
pepper slices to garnish

Halve, core and deseed the peppers. Cut the halves lengthways, sprinkle with salt and coat with the flour, egg and breadcrumbs. Deep fry in hot oil until golden brown. Garnish with slices of uncooked pepper. Serve with a potato salad as a lunch or supper dish.

Stuffed peppers

(Illustrated on page 107)

4 green peppers
225 g/8 oz pork mince
2 eggs, beaten
salt and freshly ground black pepper
50 g/2 oz butter
1 large onion, chopped
100 g/4 oz cooked ham, chopped
225 g/8 oz mushrooms, sliced

Cut the stalk ends off the peppers and remove the core and seeds. Mix the mince with the eggs and season with salt and pepper. Use

this mixture to fill the peppers. Melt the butter in a flameproof casserole and fry the onion until soft. Stir in the ham and mushrooms. Place the peppers on top of this mixture. Cover the casserole and bake in a moderately hot oven (190 C, 375 F, gas 5) for 50–60 minutes.

Creamed peppers

450 g/1 lb green or red peppers
50 g/2 oz butter
salt
150 ml/¼ pint single cream

Core and deseed the peppers, then cut into thick strips. Melt the butter and fry the peppers gently until soft. Season well with salt and pour over the cream. Heat through gently. Serve as an accompaniment to roast pork, beef or lamb.

Variation:
Creamed peppers with dill

Fry 1 small chopped onion with the peppers and stir in 2 tablespoons chopped fresh dill with the cream.

Deep-fried peppers

Baked eggs with spinach

Stuffed peppers ▶

Peppers with tomato sauce

40 g/1½ oz butter
1 medium onion, chopped
1 clove garlic, crushed
225 g/8 oz tomatoes, peeled and
    chopped
450 g/1 lb red or green peppers, cut
    into strips
salt and freshly ground black pepper

Melt the butter and fry the onion and garlic until soft. Add the tomatoes, peppers and salt and pepper to taste. Cover and simmer gently until the peppers are soft. This sauce goes well with spaghetti or other types of pasta.

Pork chops with tomatoes

50 g/2 oz butter
1 large onion, chopped
4 pork chops
25 g/1 oz plain flour
salt and freshly ground black pepper
450 g/1 lb tomatoes, peeled and
    quartered
3 tablespoons single cream
1 tablespoon chopped parsley

Melt the butter in a large frying pan or flameproof casserole and fry the onion until soft. Coat the chops with seasoned flour and add to the pan. Brown quickly on both sides. Add half the tomatoes, cover the pan and simmer gently for 30–35 minutes or until the chops are cooked through. Remove the chops to a warmed serving dish. Add the remaining tomatoes to the sauce and check the seasoning. Stir in the cream and parsley and pour the sauce over the chops. Serve with boiled rice or noodles.

Peppers with bacon

450 g/1 lb red or green peppers
100 g/4 oz streaky bacon, chopped
salt and freshly ground black pepper

Core and deseed the peppers, then cut them into strips or rings. Fry the bacon until the fat runs. Add the peppers and fry gently until tender. Season to taste with salt and pepper. This goes well with pork dishes.

Fritto misto

(Illustrated on pages 110–11)

100 g/4 oz tomatoes, sliced
100 g/4 oz peppers, deseeded and
    sliced
100 g/4 oz onion, coarsely sliced
100 g/4 oz cauliflower, broken into
    florets
100 g/4 oz celery, sliced
100 g/4 oz vegetable marrow,
    deseeded and sliced
salt
25 g/1 oz plain flour
2 eggs, beaten

50 g/2 oz dry breadcrumbs
oil for deep frying
lemon wedges for serving

Sprinkle the vegetables with salt and coat with flour. Dip in egg and breadcrumbs and fry a few pieces of vegetable at a time until golden brown. Serve with wedges of lemon and a mixed salad.

Fried marrow

(Illustrated on page 111)

1 medium marrow (vegetable or
    custard)
salt and freshly ground black pepper
25 g/1 oz plain flour
1 egg, beaten
2 tablespoons dry breadcrumbs
oil for frying

Peel and slice the marrow and remove the seeds. Sprinkle the slices with salt and pepper and dip them in flour, egg and breadcrumbs. Shallow fry in hot oil until golden brown, turning once. Serve with wedges of lemon and a mixed salad.

Peas with dill

50 g/2 oz butter
2 small onions, chopped
450 g/1 lb frozen or fresh peas
25 g/1 oz chopped dill or parsley
salt

Melt the butter and fry the onion until soft. Meanwhile blanch the peas for 2 minutes in boiling salted water. Drain the peas and add to the onion. Add the dill or parsley, season with salt and stir well. Serve as an accompaniment to lamb.

Puréed peas

675 g/1½ lb frozen or fresh peas
40 g/1½ oz butter
salt
pinch sugar (optional)

Cook the peas in boiling salted water until tender. Pass through a sieve or purée in a liquidizer or food processor. Melt the butter in a saucepan and add the purée. Heat through gently and season to taste with salt and sugar, if liked. Serve as an accompaniment to veal or pork.

Sweetcorn with peppers

75 g/3 oz streaky bacon, chopped
1 small onion, finely chopped
225 g/8 oz green peppers, deseeded
    and chopped
225 g/8 oz sweetcorn kernels
salt and freshly ground black pepper

Fry the bacon until the fat runs. Add the onion and fry until soft. Add the peppers and fry for about

5 minutes or until the peppers start to soften. Stir in the sweetcorn and a good seasoning of salt and pepper. Fry for a further 5 minutes, stirring from time to time. Serve as an accompaniment to roast chicken or use as a filling for omelettes or pancakes.

Baked tomatoes

8 medium tomatoes
salt and freshly ground black pepper
75 g/3 oz liver pâté
3 eggs, beaten
25 g/1 oz Parmesan cheese, grated
40 g/1½ oz butter

Cut the top off each tomato and remove the seeds. Season the insides and fill with pieces of pâté. Pour over the eggs mixed with the Parmesan cheese. Arrange in a greased ovenproof dish. Dot with flakes of butter and bake in a moderate oven (170 C, 325 F, gas 3) for 15–20 minutes or until the eggs are set. Serve as an accompaniment to grilled meat.

Tomato and prawn toast

40 g/1½ oz butter
2 teaspoons concentrated tomato
    purée
4 slices bread, toasted
4 medium tomatoes, sliced
salt

100 g/4 oz peeled prawns,
    defrosted, if frozen
1 tablespoon lemon juice
40 g/1½ oz Cheddar cheese, grated

Cream the butter with the tomato purée and spread on the bread. Arrange the slices of tomato on the toast and season with salt. Arrange the prawns on top and sprinkle with lemon juice. Top with grated cheese and place under a pre-heated grill until golden and bubbling. Serve at once with a green salad as a light lunch or supper dish.

French beans in batter

450 g/1 lb French beans
salt
100 g/4 oz plain flour
1 egg
150 ml/¼ pint milk
oil for deep frying

Top and tail the French beans and cook in boiling salted water for 5 minutes or until just beginning to soften. Drain well. Sift the flour and a pinch of salt into a basin. Add the egg and milk and beat until smooth. Use the batter to coat the beans and deep fry, a few at a time, in the oil until golden.

Fried marrow

◀ *Fritto misto*

Leeks with devilled sauce

(Illustrated on page 114)

50 g/2 oz butter
2 small onions, chopped
1 small red or green pepper, deseeded
  and chopped
50 g/2 oz mushrooms, sliced
2 tablespoons concentrated tomato
  purée
40 g/1½ oz black olives, stoned
25 g/1 oz capers
salt
450 g/1 lb leeks

Melt the butter and fry the onion and pepper until soft. Add the mushrooms and fry until juice runs. Stir in the tomato purée, olives, capers and salt to taste. Heat through thoroughly. While the sauce is cooking, prepare the leeks. Wash them thoroughly and boil in salted water for 10 minutes. Drain well and place in a warmed serving dish with the sauce.

Peppers with chicken ragoût

(Illustrated on page 114)

4 medium red or green peppers
50 g/2 oz butter
1 medium onion, chopped
2 chicken breasts, boned, skinned
  and diced
100 g/4 oz mushrooms, sliced
100 ml/4 fl oz single cream

salt and freshly ground black pepper
pinch freshly grated nutmeg
1 tablespoon lemon juice
Garnish (optional):
    tomato wedges, pepper rings,
    sliced mushrooms

Cut the stalk ends off the peppers and remove the core and seeds. Blanch in boiling salted water for 5 minutes. Melt the butter in a saucepan and fry the onion until soft. Add the chicken and fry over a low heat for 10–15 minutes or until cooked through and tender. Add the mushrooms and fry for a further few minutes. Pour over the cream and season with salt, pepper and nutmeg. Remove from the heat and stir in the lemon juice. Use this mixture to fill the peppers. Place the peppers in an ovenproof dish and pour over any remaining chicken mixture. Cover and bake in a moderate oven (180 C, 350 F, gas 4) for 20–25 minutes or until the peppers are tender. Garnish with tomato, pepper and mushrooms, if desired. Serve with rice.

Lettuce with mushrooms and eggs

50 g/2 oz butter
225 g/8 oz mushrooms, sliced
2 heads lettuce, shredded
salt and freshly ground black pepper
1 teaspoon caraway seeds
4 eggs, beaten

Melt the butter and fry the mush-

rooms until soft. Add the lettuce and toss in the butter until soft. Season to taste with salt, pepper and caraway seeds. Stir in the eggs and cook until set.

Lettuce with almonds

2 heads lettuce
50 g/2 oz butter
2 tablespoons chopped chives
40 g/1½ oz blanched almonds,
  chopped
salt and freshly ground black pepper
pinch freshly grated nutmeg

Halve the lettuces and cook in boiling salted water for 5 minutes. Drain and toss in melted butter for 2–3 minutes with the chives and almonds. Season with salt, pepper and nutmeg.

Lettuce stuffed with chicken

(Illustrated on page 115)

2 heads lettuce
100 g/4 oz carrots, cut into strips
225 g/8 oz cooked chicken, cut into
  strips
100 g/4 oz cooked ham, cut into
  strips
100 g/4 oz canned bamboo shoots,
  cut into strips
100 g/4 oz spring onions, chopped
salt and freshly ground black pepper
40 g/1½ oz butter
3 tablespoons oil

3 tablespoons soy sauce
1 clove garlic, crushed
pinch ground ginger

Halve the lettuces and blanch in boiling salted water for 2 minutes. Drain well and arrange on a board or work surface. Blanch the carrot in boiling water for 3 minutes and drain. Pile the carrot, chicken, ham, bamboo shoots and spring onion on the lettuce. Sprinkle with salt and roll up. Place in a greased ovenproof dish and dot with butter. Bake in a moderate oven (180 C, 350 F, gas 4) for 25 minutes. Mix together the oil, soy sauce, garlic, salt, pepper and ginger to make a dressing. Serve the stuffed lettuce with rice and hand the dressing separately.

Swiss chard with hollandaise sauce

(Illustrated on page 113)

450 g/1 lb Swiss chard ribs
1 quantity hollandaise sauce (see page 153)
Garnish:
    dill or parsley sprigs
    slices red pepper

Cook the chard in boiling salted water for 10-20 minutes until soft. Drain and arrange on a serving dish. Pour over the hollandaise sauce and garnish with slices of pepper and sprigs of dill or parsley.

Tomatoes with basil

50 g/2 oz butter
3 shallots, chopped
450 g/1 lb tomatoes, peeled and chopped
1 tablespoon fresh chopped basil or 1 teaspoon dried basil
salt and freshly ground black pepper

Melt the butter and fry the shallots until tender. Add the tomatoes, basil and salt and pepper to taste. Cook over a low heat for 5 minutes. Serve with spaghetti or noodles, or as an accompaniment to grilled lamb chops.

Stuffed onions

8 medium onions
50 g/2 oz streaky bacon, chopped
225 g/8 oz pork mince
75 g/3 oz mushrooms, chopped
50 g/2 oz fresh breadcrumbs
2 egg yolks
salt and freshly ground black pepper
100 ml/4 fl oz stock or water

Cook the peeled onions in boiling salted water for about 15 minutes until the onions are tender but not soft. Scoop out the insides and chop the flesh. Fry the bacon until the fat runs. Add the mince and fry until cooked and crumbly. Stir in the mushrooms and continue cooking until soft. Remove from the heat and stir in the bread-crumbs, onion pulp and egg yolks. Season well with salt and pepper. Stuff the onion shells with the mixture and place in a greased ovenproof dish. Pour over the stock, cover and cook in a moderate oven (180 C, 350 F, gas 4) for 45 minutes. Uncover and cook for a further 15 minutes.

Mushroom-stuffed peppers

4 large red or green peppers
40 g/1½ oz butter
1 medium onion, chopped
450 g/1 lb mushrooms
salt and freshly ground black pepper
2 eggs, beaten
40 g/1½ oz Cheddar cheese, grated

Cut the tops off the peppers and remove the core and seeds. Blanch in boiling water for 5 minutes and drain. Melt the butter and fry the onion until soft. Add the mush-rooms and cook until the juice evaporates. Season to taste with salt and pepper, then pour over the beaten eggs. Cook until the eggs are set. Use this mixture to stuff the peppers. Place the peppers in an ovenproof dish and sprinkle over the grated cheese. Bake in a moderate oven (180 C, 350 F, gas 4) until the cheese is melted and golden.

Peppers with chicken ragoût

Leeks with devilled sauce,
Swiss chard with hollandaise sauce

Lettuce stuffed with chicken ▶

Cauliflower au gratin

1 large cauliflower, broken into
    florets
salt
butter for greasing the dish
100 ml/4 fl oz single cream
4 egg yolks
100 g/4 oz Emmental cheese, grated

Cook the cauliflower in boiling
salted water for 5–10 minutes until
just tender. Arrange the cauliflower
in a greased ovenproof dish. Pour
the cream mixed with the egg yolks
and cheese over the cauliflower and
bake in a moderate oven (180 C,
350 F, gas 4) for 20–25 minutes
until set.

Stuffed tomatoes

75 g/3 oz streaky bacon, chopped
1 medium onion, chopped
8 medium tomatoes, peeled, halved
    and deseeded
1 tablespoon chopped chives
8 egg yolks
salt and freshly ground black pepper
75 g/3 oz Cheddar cheese, grated

Fry the bacon until the fat runs.
Add the onion and fry until soft.
Fill half the tomatoes with a sprinkling of chives and an egg yolk.
Fill the other half with the onion
and bacon mixture. Season with
salt and pepper to taste. Sprinkle
over the cheese and place in an
ovenproof dish. Bake in a moderately hot oven (190 C, 375 F,
gas 5) for 15–20 minutes until the
cheese is melted and golden.

Sweetcorn soufflé

350 g/12 oz sweetcorn kernels
salt and freshly ground white pepper
2 tablespoons chopped chives
4 eggs, separated
2 tablespoons double cream
butter for greasing the dish

Cook the sweetcorn in boiling water
until soft and pass through a sieve
or purée in a liquidizer or food
processor. Season with salt and
pepper, add the chopped chives,
egg yolks and cream. Whisk the
egg whites until stiff and fold into
the purée. Turn into a greased
soufflé dish and bake in a moderate
oven (180 C, 350 F, gas 4) for
30–35 minutes until well-risen and
golden brown.

Mange tout with prawns

40 g/1½ oz butter
2 shallots, chopped
450 g/1 lb mange tout or sugar peas,
    topped and tailed
225 g/8 oz peeled prawns, defrosted
    if frozen
salt and freshly ground black pepper
juice of ½ lemon
2 tablespoons chopped parsley

Melt the butter in a large frying
pan and fry the shallots until soft.
Add the mange tout or sugar peas
and continue frying, stirring frequently, until they just begin to
soften. Add the prawns and cook
until just heated through. Season
to taste with salt, pepper and lemon
juice. Finally stir in the chopped
parsley.

Buttered corn cobs

(Illustrated on page 118)

50 g/2 oz butter
4 young cobs of corn
    or 1 (397-g/14-oz) can
    miniature corn cobs
salt and freshly ground black pepper
Garnish:
    2 tomatoes, peeled and halved
    4 sprigs parsley

Melt the butter in a large frying
pan and toss the corn cobs over
a medium heat until cooked. Time
taken will vary with size and age
of the cobs. Season well with salt
and a little pepper. Serve garnished
with the tomato halves and sprigs
of parsley.

Creamed lettuce

(Illustrated on page 118)

2 heads lettuce
1 small onion, chopped
50 g/2 oz butter

25 g/2 oz plain flour
3 tablespoons chicken stock
salt and freshly ground white pepper
100 g/4 oz cooked ham, cut into
    strips
3 tablespoons double cream
few drops lemon juice
Garnish:
    1 hard-boiled egg, sieved
    lettuce leaves
    tomato wedges

Wash and quarter the lettuce. Blanch for 2 minutes in boiling salted water. Drain. Fry the finely chopped onion in the butter. Stir in the flour, stock and salt and pepper to taste. Add the lettuce and braise for 5–7 minutes. Add the ham and stir in the cream. Cook for 2–3 minutes and add lemon juice to taste. Garnish with hardboiled egg, fresh lettuce leaves and wedges of tomato.

Tomatoes with spaghetti

(Illustrated on page 119)

225 g/8 oz spaghetti
40 g/1½ oz butter
salt and freshly ground black pepper
450 g/1 lb tomatoes, peeled and
    quartered
100 g/4 oz Emmental cheese, grated
parsley sprigs to garnish

Cook the spaghetti in boiling salted water until just tender. Drain well and return to the pan with the butter. Season well and toss the spaghetti gently. Stir in the tomatoes. Turn into a flameproof serving dish and top with the cheese. Place under a preheated hot grill until the cheese is golden and bubbling. Serve at once garnished with parsley.

Radishes with ham and eggs

1 large bunch radishes
1 medium onion, chopped
50 g/2 oz butter
salt and freshly ground black pepper
100 g/4 oz cooked ham, diced
4 eggs, beaten

Slice the radishes and fry them with the onion in the butter over a medium heat. Add salt and pepper to taste and cook over a low heat for 8–10 minutes. Add the ham and stir in the eggs. Cook until the eggs are set. Serve with crusty French bread or buttered new potatoes.

Puréed cauliflower

1 large cauliflower, broken into
    florets
40 g/1½ oz butter
salt and freshly ground white pepper
pinch freshly grated nutmeg
3 tablespoons single cream

Cook the cauliflower in boiling salted water until tender. Drain well and press through a sieve or purée in a blender or food processor. Melt the butter and add the purée. Heat through gently and season to taste with salt, pepper and nutmeg. Add the cream just before serving.

Variation:
Puréed cauliflower with cheese

Add 100 g/4 oz grated cheese (Cheddar or Emmental) to the re-heated purée. Stir until the cheese dissolves. Omit the cream.

Kohlrabi with paprika

40 g/1½ oz butter
2 small onions, chopped
2 teaspoons paprika
4 large kohlrabis, diced
salt
100 ml/4 fl oz stock or water
150 ml/¼ pint single or soured cream

Melt the butter and fry the onion until soft. Stir in the paprika and fry for 1–2 minutes. Add the kohlrabi, salt to taste and stock or water. Cover the pan and simmer for 20–30 minutes or until the kohlrabi is tender. Stir in the cream and serve at once as an accompaniment to roast lamb or beef.

Creamed lettuce

Buttered corn cobs

Tomatoes with spaghetti ▶

Pancakes
with vegetable filling

(Illustrated on page 122)

Batter:
100 g/4 oz plain flour
pinch salt
1 egg, beaten
300 ml/½ pint milk
oil for frying
Filling:
100 g/4 oz peppers, deseeded and
  sliced
100 g/4 oz mushrooms, sliced
1 large onion, sliced
75 g/3 oz butter
salt and freshly ground black pepper
100 g/4 oz tomatoes, sliced
50 g/2 oz Cheddar cheese, grated
Garnish:
  1 tablespoon chopped parsley
  pepper rings
  dill or parsley sprigs

To make the pancakes, sift the flour and salt into a basin. Make a well in the centre and add the egg and milk. Mix well to make a smooth batter. Heat the oil in a frying pan and make four pancakes, keep warm. Fry the peppers, mushrooms and onion separately in butter until soft. Season to taste with salt and pepper. Layer the pancakes and vegetables in a greased ovenproof dish. Top with the sliced tomatoes and sprinkle over the cheese. Bake in a moderately hot oven (190 C, 375 F, gas 5) for about 30 minutes or until the cheese is melted. Sprinkle over the parsley and garnish with the pepper rings and sprigs of dill or parsley. Cut into wedges to serve.

Vegetable-stuffed
artichokes

8 canned artichoke bottoms
25 g/1 oz butter
225 g/8 oz mixed cooked vegetables
  (e.g. carrots, cauliflower, peas)
salt and freshly ground black pepper

Warm up the artichokes in the liquid from the can. Arrange in a serving dish and keep warm. Melt the butter and sauté the vegetables until thoroughly heated. Season to taste with salt and pepper. Fill the artichokes with the vegetable mixture and serve with bread as a light main dish or as an accompaniment to roast beef or lamb.

Russian dill pancakes

(Illustrated on page 123)

Pancakes:
450 g/1 lb curd cheese or quark
100 g/4 oz semolina
2 eggs, beaten
pinch salt
4 tablespoons finely chopped dill or
  parsley
oil for frying
Topping:
150 ml/¼ pint soured cream

smoked salmon, caviar or lumpfish
  roe, crabmeat
Garnish:
  1 lemon, finely sliced
  dill or parsley sprigs

Mix the curd cheese or quark with the semolina, eggs, salt and parsley. Form into small flat pancakes and shallow fry in hot oil, turning once. Top with soured cream and smoked salmon, caviar or lumpfish roe, or crabmeat. Garnish with slices of lemon and sprigs of dill or parsley.

Chinese peas with ham

450 g/1 lb frozen or fresh peas
2 tablespoons finely chopped
  shallots or spring onions
3 tablespoons butter
slice cooked ham
soy sauce
salt and freshly ground black pepper

Place the peas, shallots or spring onions and half the butter in a shallow dish or bowl and steam over boiling water in a covered saucepan or double boiler for 10–15 minutes, until tender. Cut the cooked ham into strips and sauté in the remaining butter. Mix in the steamed peas and season to taste with a little soy sauce and salt and pepper.

Stir-fried Savoy cabbage

1 medium Savoy cabbage
4 tablespoons oil
1 clove garlic, crushed
175 g/6 oz cashew nuts
75 g/3 oz dates, stoned and chopped
2 tablespoons white wine vinegar
2 teaspoons Dijon mustard

Finely shred the cabbage. Heat the oil in a wok and add the garlic. Mix in the cabbage, cashew nuts and dates, then stir-fry for 2–3 minutes. Stir in the vinegar and mustard and continue stirring for 1–2 minutes. Serve immediately.

Stir-braised vegetables with almonds

1 small cauliflower
225 g/8 oz carrots
1 large green pepper
1 onion
2 tablespoons soy sauce
1 tablespoon cornflour
300 ml/½ pint chicken stock
3 tablespoons oil
1 clove garlic, crushed
100 g/4 oz blanched almonds
1 teaspoon ground ginger

Separate the cauliflower into florets. Thinly slice the carrots. Core and deseed the pepper and cut into strips. Thinly slice the onion. Mix the soy sauce with the cornflour and stock. Heat the oil in a wok and add the garlic. Add the almonds, cauliflower, carrots, pepper and onion. Sprinkle the ground ginger over the vegetables and stir-fry for 2–3 minutes. Pour the soy sauce mixture into the pan and bring to the boil, stirring all the time. Cover the wok and cook the vegetables for 10 minutes, until tender.

Stir-fried mange tout

450 g/1 lb mange tout or sugar peas
3 tablespoons oil
2 cloves garlic
4 tablespoons dry sherry
2 tablespoons soy sauce

Top and tail the mange tout, if necessary. Heat the oil in a wok, then add the mange tout and whole cloves of peeled garlic. Stir-fry for 2–3 minutes. Remove the garlic and add the sherry and soy sauce. Lower the heat and continue to stir-fry for 1–2 minutes.

Stir-fried broccoli

450 g/1 lb broccoli
3 tablespoons oil
3 tablespoons water
½ teaspoon salt
¼ teaspoon sugar

Trim the broccoli, cutting off any leaves and any thick, tough stalks, and cut into 5-cm/2-in pieces. Heat the oil in a wok, then add the broccoli. Stir-fry for 2–3 minutes. Add the water, salt and sugar and mix in well. Lower the heat and continue to stir-fry for about 5 minutes, until the broccoli is tender but still crisp.

◀ *Pancakes with vegetable filling*

Russian dill pancakes

Sweetcorn with black olives

French beans with bacon and tomatoes

225 g/8 oz French beans
100 g/4 oz streaky bacon, chopped
225 g/8 oz tomatoes, peeled and
    chopped
1 tablespoon chopped chives
salt and freshly ground black pepper

Top and tail the beans and string if necessary. If large, cut into two or three pieces. Blanch the beans in boiling water for 2–3 minutes, then drain. Fry the bacon until the fat runs, add the beans and toss for 2–3 minutes. Stir in the tomatoes and chives and heat through. Season to taste with pepper and a little extra salt, if necessary.

Variation:

French beans with tomato and onion

(Illustrated on page 126)

Add 1 coarsely chopped onion to the melted bacon fat and fry until soft before adding the French beans. Add 100 ml/4 fl oz tomato juice with the tomatoes.

Sweetcorn with black olives

(Illustrated on page·123)

450 g/1 lb sweetcorn kernels
40 g/1½ oz butter
16 black olives, stoned
salt and freshly ground black pepper

Cook the sweetcorn in boiling salted water until tender, then drain. Melt the butter in the saucepan and add the sweetcorn, olives and salt and pepper to taste. Heat gently for 1–2 minutes. Serve as an accompaniment to pork chops with a mixed salad.

Buttered vegetables with ham

(Illustrated on pages 126–7)

50 g/2 oz butter
75 g/3 oz cooked ham, chopped
675 g/1½ lb cooked mixed vegetables
    (e.g. cauliflower, carrots, peas,
    Brussels sprouts)
salt and freshly ground black pepper

Melt the butter and fry the ham for a few minutes until heated through. Add the vegetables and salt and pepper to taste and sauté over medium heat until piping hot. Serve as a complete meal with boiled potatoes or use as an omelette filling.

Cauliflower ragoût

(Illustrated on page 126)

1 large cauliflower
1 small onion, finely chopped
75 g/3 oz butter
50 g/2 oz plain flour
salt and freshly ground black pepper
pinch ground mace
250 ml/8 fl oz stock
225 g/8 oz button mushrooms
100 ml/4 fl oz double cream
2 egg yolks
1 tablespoon lemon juice
2 tablespoons chopped parsley

Divide the cauliflower into florets and cook in boiling salted water until just tender. Fry the finely chopped onion in half the butter until soft. Stir in the flour, add salt and pepper to taste and a pinch of mace. Fry briefly, add the stock and cook until the sauce thickens. Wipe the mushrooms and fry in the remaining butter, adding salt to taste. Strain the sauce over the mushrooms. Add the cream, egg yolks and cauliflower. Heat through thoroughly without boiling. Remove from the heat, stir in the lemon juice and parsley and serve at once.

Onions au gratin

8 medium onions
50 g/2 oz butter
50 g/2 oz plain flour
100 ml/4 fl oz milk
100 ml/4 fl oz single cream
salt
pinch ground mace
2 egg yolks
100 g/4 oz Cheddar cheese, grated

Cook the peeled onions in boiling salted water for 15–20 minutes until tender. Drain, cool slightly and slice into thick rings or quarters. Arrange in a flameproof dish. Melt the butter in a saucepan, stir in the flour and cook for 1–2 minutes. Add the milk and cream and cook until the sauce thickens. Season to taste with salt and mace. Remove from the heat and stir in the egg yolks. Pour the sauce over the onions, scatter the cheese over the top and place under a preheated grill until golden and bubbling.

Creamed French beans

(Illustrated on page 126)

450 g/1 lb French beans
100 g/4 oz button mushrooms
65 g/2½ oz butter
40 g/1½ oz plain flour
150 ml/¼ pint single cream or creamy milk
salt and freshly ground black pepper
1 tablespoon chopped parsley

Top and tail the French beans and cook in boiling salted water for 5–8 minutes until just tender. Drain well. Wipe the mushrooms and fry gently in 25 g/1 oz of the butter until the juice runs. Melt the remaining butter in another saucepan and stir in the flour. Add the cream or milk and cook until the sauce thickens. Season with salt and pepper to taste. Add the mushrooms with their juice and the beans. Heat through, turn into a serving dish and sprinkle with parsley. Serve

with a salad as a light summer supper.

Vegetable curry

(Illustrated on page 127)

100 g/4 oz carrots, diced
100 g/4 oz kohlrabi, diced
100 g/4 oz frozen or fresh peas
100 g/4 oz frozen sweetcorn kernels or canned miniature corn cobs
40 g/1½ oz butter
40 g/1½ oz plain flour
1 tablespoon curry powder
100 ml/4 fl oz double cream
salt and freshly ground white pepper

Cook the vegetables in boiling salted water until tender. Drain, reserving the cooking liquid. Melt the butter and stir in the flour and curry powder. Cook for 1–2 minutes, stirring. Add 300 ml/½ pint of the vegetable stock. Bring to the boil and stir in the cream with extra salt and pepper, if required. Add the cooked vegetables to the sauce and reheat gently. Serve with rice or as an accompaniment to chicken.

Brussels sprouts with bacon

(Illustrated on pages 126–7)

675 g/1½ lb Brussels sprouts
2 large onions, chopped
100 g/4 oz streaky bacon, chopped

3 tablespoons oil
salt and freshly ground black pepper
1–2 teaspoons sugar
1–2 teaspoons vinegar
Garnish (optional):
    strips of ham
    shredded carrot

Trim the Brussels sprouts and cook in boiling salted water for about 5 minutes until tender. Drain well. Lightly fry the onion and bacon in the oil and mix with the sprouts. Season with salt, pepper, sugar and vinegar to taste and garnish with ham and carrots, if desired.

Spinach with ham

225 g/8 oz spinach
75 g/3 oz streaky bacon, chopped
1 large onion, chopped
1 clove garlic, crushed
100 g/4 oz cooked ham, chopped
salt and freshly ground black pepper

Wash the spinach and blanch in boiling water for 2–3 minutes. Drain and chop coarsely. Fry the bacon until the fat runs, then add the onion and garlic and fry until soft. Add the ham and cook until heated through. Finally add the spinach and season to taste with salt and pepper. Cook gently for a few minutes. Use as an accompaniment to meat dishes or as a filling for omelettes.

Vegetable curry

◀

Creamed French beans, French beans with tomato and onion, Brussels sprouts with bacon, Buttered vegetables with ham, Cauliflower ragoût

Fried stuffed onions

75 g/3 oz Camembert cheese
2 egg yolks
75 g/3 oz cooked ham, chopped
salt and freshly ground black pepper
450 g/1 lb onions
1 tablespoon plain flour
1 egg, beaten
2 tablespoons dry breadcrumbs
oil for frying

Remove the rind from the Camembert and mash well, add the egg yolks and ham, salt and pepper to taste and mix well. Slice the onions into thick rings, spread them with the stuffing and make onion sandwiches. Coat them with flour, egg and breadcrumbs, and shallow fry in the oil until golden brown. Be careful when turning them not to let the 'sandwiches' slide apart. A suitable side-dish for steak or lamb chops.

Onions with raisins

450 g/1 lb pickling onions
50 g/2 oz butter
salt and freshly ground black pepper
100 g/4 oz raisins
100 ml/4 fl oz white wine
pinch dried thyme

Fry the onions in the butter. Add salt and pepper to taste and the raisins and wine. Simmer for 5–10 minutes, until the sauce is reduced by half. Cool and chill in the refrigerator.

Stuffed fennel

(Illustrated on page 130)

2 medium bulbs fennel
4 tablespoons oil
1 tablespoon vinegar
salt and freshly ground white pepper
450 g/1 lb lightly cooked mixed
    vegetables
Garnish:
    black olives
    parsley sprigs

Separate the layers of the fennel bulbs and blanch in boiling salted water to which a dash of vinegar has been added, for 5 minutes. Drain well and place in a bowl. Whisk the oil and vinegar with salt and pepper to taste and pour over the fennel. Marinate for 2 hours. Fill the pieces of fennel with the vegetables and garnish with black olives and sprigs of parsley. Serve with grilled meat.

Radishes with caraway

(Illustrated on page 130)

1 large bunch radishes
1 medium onion, chopped
50 g/2 oz butter
salt and white pepper
1–2 teaspoons caraway seeds

Peel and slice the radishes. Lightly fry the onion in the butter. Add the radishes, salt, pepper and caraway seeds and cook gently until just beginning to soften. Serve as an accompaniment to meat, or as an omelette filling.

Creamed radishes

(Illustrated on page 130)

1 large bunch radishes
small bunch spring onions, chopped
50 g/2 oz butter
salt and white pepper
3 tablespoons double cream
1 egg yolk
1 teaspoon lemon juice

Wash, trim and quarter the radishes. Lightly fry the chopped spring onion in the butter. Add the radishes, salt and pepper and cook gently until just tender. Stir in the cream blended with the egg yolk, heat through (without boiling) and add the lemon juice. Serve with boiled potatoes.

Stuffed peppers
in cream sauce

(Illustrated on page 131)

4 medium green peppers
225 g/8 oz cooked beef or lamb,
    minced
100 g/4 oz cooked rice
1 egg, beaten
salt and freshly ground black pepper

1 medium onion, chopped
50 g/2 oz butter
150 g/6 oz tomatoes, chopped
4 tablespoons double cream
parsley sprig to garnish

Core and deseed the peppers. Mix the meat, rice and egg with salt and pepper to taste to make the stuffing and fill the peppers. Fry the onion in the butter until soft and add the tomatoes. Place this mixture in an ovenproof dish and top with the peppers. Bake in a moderately hot oven (190 C, 375 F, gas 5) for 40 minutes. Stir the cream into the tomato sauce and serve the dish hot with rice, garnished with a sprig of parsley.

Tomato and onion omelette

75 g/3 oz streaky bacon, chopped
225 g/8 oz onions, chopped
225 g/8 oz tomatoes, peeled and chopped
8 eggs
salt and freshly ground black pepper
40 g/1½ oz butter for frying the omelettes

Fry the bacon until the fat runs, add the onion and fry until browned. Stir in the tomatoes. Keep the filling warm while you make four omelettes out of the eggs beaten with salt and pepper to taste. Divide the filling between the four omelettes, fold over and slide onto a warmed plate. Serve with a green salad and fresh bread rolls.

Deep-fried onion rings

350 g/12 oz large onions
2 tablespoons plain flour
2 eggs, beaten
4 tablespoons dry breadcrumbs
oil for deep frying
salt
1 tablespoon chopped parsley

Slice the onions into rounds and divide into separate rings. Dip the rings in the flour, egg and breadcrumbs and deep fry a few at a time in the oil. Drain on absorbent kitchen paper. Season with salt and sprinkle with chopped parsley. Serve with grilled steak, chops, etc.

Tomatoes with chicken liver

100 g/4 oz streaky bacon, chopped
1 medium onion, chopped
450 g/1 lb chicken livers, sliced
salt and freshly ground black pepper
225 g/8 oz tomatoes, chopped
2 tablespoons dry breadcrumbs
75 g/3 oz Emmental cheese, grated

Fry the bacon until the fat runs, then add the onion and fry until soft. Add the chicken livers, season to taste and sauté over a medium heat until cooked through. Turn the liver into a greased flameproof dish and top with the tomatoes. Mix together the breadcrumbs and the cheese and sprinkle them over the tomatoes. Place under a pre-heated grill until the topping is golden.

Baked and stuffed tomatoes

100 g/4 oz cold roast meat (beef, lamb, pork)
1 medium onion, chopped
40 g/1½ oz butter
salt and freshly ground black pepper
2 egg yolks
3 tablespoons double cream
8 medium tomatoes, deseeded
2 tablespoons chopped chives to garnish

Cut the roast meat into small cubes and fry with the onion in the butter until the onion is soft. Add salt and pepper to taste and the egg yolks mixed with the cream. Allow the mixture to thicken and use to fill the tomato shells. Place in an ovenproof dish and bake in a moderately hot oven (190 C, 375 F, gas 5) for 20–25 minutes. Scatter over the chives before serving.

Stuffed fennel

Creamed radishes,
Radishes with caraway

Stuffed peppers in cream sauce ▶

Baked onions with garlic

225 g/8 oz onions, sliced
4 cloves garlic, very finely sliced
150 g/6 oz cooked ham, thinly sliced
salt and freshly ground black pepper
4 eggs

Cut four (20-cm/8-in) squares out of aluminium foil. Divide the onion, garlic and ham between them and season with salt and pepper to taste. Break an egg over each one and fold up the parcels, being careful not to break the eggs. Put into a hot oven (220 C, 425 F, gas 7) for 10 minutes. Alternatively place on a barbecue for 10 minutes.

Spinach gnocchi

(Illustrated on page 134)

100 g/4 oz butter
100 ml/4 fl oz salted water
50 g/2 oz plain flour
50 g/2 oz semolina
2 eggs
225 g/8 oz cooked spinach, chopped
salt and freshly ground black pepper
50 g/2 oz Cheddar cheese, grated

Put the butter into the salted water and bring to the boil. Gradually stir in the flour and semolina and mix to make a smooth paste. Cool slightly, stir in the eggs, spinach and salt and pepper to taste. Form

small dumplings and cook them in boiling salted water for 20 minutes. Drain and scatter over the cheese. Serve as a light meal or as an accompaniment to a casserole.

Spinach pancakes

(Illustrated on page 134)

675 g/1½ lb spinach
1 small onion, finely chopped
1 clove garlic, crushed
25 g/1 oz butter
25 g/1 oz plain flour
100 ml/4 fl oz milk
salt and freshly ground black pepper
4 eggs, separated
oil for frying
Garnish:
    150 ml/¼ pint soured cream
    slices of tomato
    slices of cucumber
    few anchovy fillets (optional)

Blanch the spinach in boiling water for 3–4 minutes until tender. Drain well and chop finely. Lightly fry the finely chopped onion and garlic in the butter until soft. Stir in the flour, fry briefly, then add the milk. Cook until the sauce thickens. Add the spinach and season with salt and pepper. Cool slightly and mix in the egg yolks. Whisk the egg whites until stiff and fold into the sauce. Heat the oil in a frying pan and drop spoonfuls of the mixture in. Cook until browned on both sides. Garnish each pancake with a spoonful of soured cream, slices

of tomato and cucumber and a small piece of anchovy, if liked.

Spinach noodles

(Illustrated on page 135)

200 g/7 oz plain flour
pinch salt
2 eggs
75 g/3 oz cooked spinach, chopped
40 g/1½ oz butter, melted
3 tablespoons double cream
50 g/2 oz Emmental or Parmesan
    cheese, grated
1 tomato, sliced, to garnish

Sift the flour and salt together and make a well in the centre. Add the eggs and spinach. Mix to a smooth dough. If the spinach makes the dough too sticky add a little extra flour. Roll out very thinly or feed through the rollers of a pasta machine. Leave to dry for at least 30 minutes, then cut into noodles. Cook in boiling salted water for a few minutes until just soft. Drain and toss immediately in the butter. Turn into a warmed serving dish and top with the cream and cheese. Garnish with slices of tomato.

Seafood chicory

4 heads chicory
50 g/2 oz butter
2 small onions, chopped
100 g/4 oz prawns, lobster or crab-
    meat, defrosted if frozen

1 tablespoon concentrated tomato
 purée
salt and freshly ground black pepper
2 tablespoons double cream
2–3 teaspoons lemon juice

Cook the chicory in boiling salted water for 20–30 minutes until tender. Drain and place in a warmed serving dish. While the chicory is cooking make the sauce. Melt the butter and fry the onion until soft. Add the seafood, tomato purée and salt and pepper to taste and heat through gently. Stir in the cream and lemon juice and pour the sauce over the chicory. Serve with rice and mushrooms or with potato croquettes.

Fried pumpkin

450 g/1 lb pumpkin
salt and freshly ground black pepper
2 tablespoons plain flour
1 egg, beaten
2 tablespoons dry breadcrumbs
oil for frying

Clean and peel the pumpkin and slice into approximately 50 g/2 oz portions. Sprinkle with salt and pepper, dip in the flour, egg and breadcrumbs, and shallow fry in the oil until golden brown.

Onions with dill

(Illustrated on page 139)

450 g/1 lb onions, chopped
2 teaspoons vinegar

25 g/1 oz butter
salt
4 tablespoons single cream
2 tablespoons chopped dill or parsley
tomato wedges to garnish

Place the onions in a saucepan. cover with water, add the vinegar and simmer for about 10 minutes until soft. Drain well and return to the pan with the butter. Stir gently until the butter melts. Add salt to taste and stir in the cream and dill or, parsley. Serve garnished with wedges of tomato.

Chicory with ham and cheese

4 heads chicory
salt
4 (25-g/1-oz) slices cooked ham
4 slices Edam cheese

Cook the chicory in a small quantity of salted water for 20–30 minutes. Drain and arrange in a greased flameproof dish. Place a slice of ham and a slice of cheese round each head of chicory. Place under a preheated grill until the cheese melts.

Chicory with chicken

4 portions boned chicken breast
40 g/1½ oz butter

2 large leeks, sliced
4 heads chicory
salt
1 tablespoon lemon juice
1 quantity cheese sauce (see page
 149)

Skin the chicken breasts and cut the meat into strips. Melt the butter and fry the leeks until beginning to soften. Add the chicken and fry until cooked and tender. Divide the chicory into leaves and cook in boiling salted water with the lemon juice for about 10 minutes until tender. Drain well and arrange half the chicory leaves in a greased flameproof dish. Top with the chicken mixture, then add the remaining chicory leaves. Pour over the cheese sauce, then place under a preheated grill until golden brown.

Chicory with mushrooms

4 heads chicory
50 g/2 oz butter
2 small onions, chopped
100 g/4 oz cooked ham, chopped
175 g/6 oz mushrooms, sliced
salt and freshly ground black pepper

Cook the chicory in just enough boiling salted water to cover for 20–30 minutes. Drain and keep warm. Melt the butter and fry the onion until soft. Add the ham and mushrooms and cook until the juice runs. Season to taste and pour the mixture over the chicory.

Sweetcorn croquettes

225 g/8 oz sweetcorn kernels
50 g/2 oz butter
40 g/1½ oz plain flour
250 ml/8 fl oz milk
salt and white pepper
4 egg yolks
1 tablespoon flour
1 egg, beaten
2 tablespoons dry breadcrumbs
oil for frying

Cook the corn for about 5 minutes in boiling salted water, then sieve or purée in a liquidizer or food processor. Melt the butter, add the flour and stir until smooth. Pour in the milk and cook until the sauce thickens. Season well with salt and pepper. Mix in the egg yolks and puréed sweetcorn. Spread the mixture in a shallow dish or baking tin and chill until firm. Cut into squares, dip in the flour, egg and breadcrumbs, and shallow fry until golden brown on both sides.

Onion quiche

(Illustrated on page 138)

225 g/8 oz shortcrust pastry
225 g/8 oz streaky bacon, chopped

◀ *Spinach gnocchi and pancakes*
Spinach noodles

225 g/8 oz onions, chopped
300 ml/½ pint milk or half milk, half single cream
2 eggs, beaten
salt and white pepper
Garnish (optional):
　tomato wedges
　1 sprig parsley
　cooked rasher bacon

Line a 20-cm/8-in flan tin with pastry. Prick the base and bake blind in a moderately hot oven (200 C, 400 F, gas 6) for 15 minutes. Fry the bacon until the fat runs and add the onion. Fry until soft. Place the onion mixture in the pastry case and pour over the milk beaten with the eggs and seasoned with salt and pepper. Reduce the oven temperature to moderate (170 C, 325 F, gas 3) and bake for 20–25 minutes until set. Garnish with the tomato, parsley and bacon, if desired.

Tomatoes with saffron rice stuffing

(Illustrated on page 138)

40 g/1½ oz butter
1 small onion, finely chopped
pinch powdered saffron
150 g/5 oz cooked rice
salt
4 large tomatoes, deseeded

Melt the butter in a small saucepan and fry the onion until soft. Stir in a pinch of saffron, the rice and

salt to taste. Cook over a low heat until hot. Use this mixture to fill the hollowed out tomatoes. Place the tomatoes in an ovenproof dish and bake in a moderately hot oven (190 C, 375 F, gas 5) for 20 minutes. Serve with grilled meat and a green salad.

Onions braised in beer

(Illustrated on page 139)

450 g/1 lb onions
100 ml/4 fl oz beer
salt
1 tablespoon chopped chives
tomato wedges to garnish

Peel the onions and slice into rings. Place in a bowl and pour over boiling water to cover. Leave for a minute, then drain. Place the onions in a saucepan, pour over the beer and season to taste with salt. Simmer for 5–10 minutes until the onions are tender. Stir in the chives and serve garnished with wedges of tomato.

Onions with honey

(Illustrated on page 139)

450 g/1 lb pickling onions
1 tablespoon vinegar
40 g/1½ oz butter
25 g/1 oz sugar
2 tablespoons honey
pinch ground ginger
salt

2 tablespoons white wine
slices green pepper to garnish

Place the onions in a saucepan and cover with water. Add the vinegar, bring to the boil and simmer until the onions are tender. Melt the butter and sugar in a frying pan, add the honey, ground ginger and salt to taste. Finally add the white wine. Cook the onions in this mixture for a few minutes, stirring so that they are well coated. Serve garnished with slices of green pepper.

Mushroom-stuffed kohlrabi

8 small kohlrabis
2 small onions, chopped
50 g/2 oz dripping or lard
225 g/8 oz mushrooms, chopped
salt and freshly ground black pepper
5 eggs, beaten
50 g/2 oz Cheddar cheese, grated

Cut the tops off the kohlrabis and scoop out the insides. Cook the shells in boiling water for 15–20 minutes until tender. Drain well. Fry the onion in the dripping or lard and add the mushrooms. Cook until soft and season to taste with salt and pepper. Pour over the eggs and cook until set. Fill the kohlrabis with this mixture and cover with the lids. Arrange them in a greased ovenproof dish and sprinkle with the grated cheese. Bake in a moderately hot oven

(200 C, 400 F, gas 6) until the cheese is melted and golden.

Baked kohlrabi with potatoes

1 large onion, chopped
25 g/1 oz dripping or lard
225 g/8 oz cooked ham, chopped
450 g/1 lb kohlrabi, thinly sliced
225 g/8 oz potatoes, thinly sliced
salt and freshly ground black pepper
3 eggs, beaten
150 ml/$\frac{1}{4}$ pint single cream or milk

Fry the onion in the fat until soft. Stir in the ham and heat through. Arrange layers of kohlrabi, potato and the onion mixture in a greased ovenproof dish, seasoning with salt and pepper as you go. Finish with a layer of potatoes. Bake in a moderately hot oven (190 C, 375 F, gas 5) for 30 minutes. Mix together the eggs and cream, pour over the vegetables and continue baking for a further 20–25 minutes until set and golden.

Vegetable purée

150 g/5 oz cauliflower florets
150 g/5 oz French beans
75 g/3 oz carrots
50 g/2 oz celeriac
50 g/2 oz butter
40 g/1$\frac{1}{2}$ oz plain flour
150 ml/$\frac{1}{4}$ pint single cream or milk

salt and freshly ground black pepper
2 egg yolks

Cook the vegetables in boiling water until tender. Sieve or purée in a liquidizer or food processor. Melt the butter, stir in the flour to make a smooth paste and add the cream or milk. Cook until the sauce thickens. Season well with salt and pepper. Stir in the egg yolks and vegetable purée and heat through gently. Serve the purée with veal or lamb or use as an omelette filling.

Kohlrabi au gratin

4 large kohlrabis
salt
50 g/2 oz butter
2 egg yolks
100 g/4 oz Cheddar cheese, grated

Cut the kohlrabis into thick slices and cook in boiling salted water for about 15 minutes or until almost soft. Grease an ovenproof dish with 15 g/$\frac{1}{2}$ oz of the butter and arrange the kohlrabis in the dish. Mix the egg yolks with the grated cheese and place on top of the kohlrabis. Melt the remaining butter and drizzle over the top. Bake in a moderate oven (180 C, 350 F, gas 4) for 25 minutes until the cheese is melted and golden. Serve with boiled potatoes and salad.

Onion quiche

Tomatoes with saffron rice stuffing

Onions braised in beer, Onions ▶
with honey, Onions with dill

Creamy marrow

(Illustrated on page 142)

450 g/1 lb peeled marrow, deseeded
   and diced
1 large onion, chopped
50 g/2 oz butter
salt and freshly ground black pepper
1–2 tablespoons lemon juice
100 ml/4 fl oz double or soured
   cream
Garnish (optional):
   parsley sprig
   100 ml/4 fl oz extra whipped
     cream

Salt the marrow and leave for
5 minutes. Press gently to squeeze
out the excess water. Lightly fry
the onion in the butter, add the
marrow and pepper to taste and
cook gently until the marrow is
tender. Add a little lemon juice to
taste and swirl in the cream. Remove
from the heat and garnish with the
parsley and whipped cream, if liked.

Marrow with paprika

(Illustrated on page 142)

1 medium onion, chopped
4 tablespoons oil
1 teaspoon paprika
450 g/1 lb marrow, peeled, deseeded
   and diced
salt
2 teaspoons caraway seeds (optional)
1–2 teaspoons wine vinegar
red pepper rings to garnish

Fry the onion in the oil, sprinkle
over the paprika and add the marrow. Sauté gently for 8–10 minutes
until tender. Season with salt, caraway and vinegar. Garnish with
rings of red pepper and serve with
roast pork or grilled pork chops.

Sweetcorn
with cream sauce

(Illustrated on page 143)

4 sweetcorn cobs
25 g/1 oz butter
1 small onion, chopped
2 egg yolks
1 tablespoon cornflour
4 tablespoons single cream
300 ml/½ pint milk
salt and freshly ground black pepper
1–2 teaspoons lemon juice
½ teaspoon dried or 1 teaspoon fresh
   chopped tarragon
red pepper slices to garnish

Cook the corn cobs in boiling
salted water for 10 minutes or until
tender. Drain and keep warm. Melt
the butter and fry the onion until
soft. Add the egg yolks to the
cornflour, then blend in the cream
and milk and pour over the onion.
Bring the sauce slowly to the boil
and remove from the heat. Season
to taste and stir in the lemon juice
and tarragon. Pour the sauce over
the sweetcorn. Garnish with slices
of red pepper.

Vegetable rice with spices

(Illustrated on page 143)

1 small onion, chopped
50 g/2 oz butter
225 g/8 oz rice
100 g/4 oz potatoes, diced
100 g/4 oz runner beans, chopped
450 ml/¾ pint chicken or vegetable
   stock
6 black peppercorns
3 cloves
salt
juice of ½ lemon
100 g/4 oz tomatoes, chopped
1 tablespoon chopped parsley

Fry the onion in the butter until
soft. Add the rice, potatoes and
beans to the fried onion, stir in the
stock and add the peppercorns,
cloves and salt to taste. Bring to
the boil, cover the pan closely and
leave to simmer on a very low heat
for 15–20 minutes until all the
liquid is absorbed. Add the lemon
juice and stir in the tomatoes and
parsley. Serve with chicken.

Courgettes with walnuts

10 small courgettes
1 tablespoon olive oil
2 tablespoons butter
50 g/2 oz walnuts, coarsely chopped
salt and freshly ground black pepper

Cut the courgettes into thin slices. Sauté in the oil and butter until almost tender. Add the chopped walnuts and salt and pepper to taste, then continue cooking over a low heat until done.

Courgettes with mint

450 g/1 lb courgettes
50 g/2 oz butter
freshly ground black pepper
1 tablespoon finely chopped mint

Slice the courgettes thickly. Add to a saucepan of boiling salted water, simmer for 2–3 minutes, then drain. Melt the butter in a large frying pan and add the courgettes. Cover and fry gently for 10–15 minutes, until tender. Season to taste with the freshly ground black pepper and sprinkle with the fresh mint.

Spinach-stuffed mushrooms

24 open button mushrooms or
    12 flat mushrooms
4 shallots, finely chopped
1 clove garlic, crushed
225 g/8 oz cooked spinach,
    drained and chopped
generous pinch dried thyme or
    $\frac{1}{2}$ teaspoon fresh thyme
1 egg, beaten
4 tablespoons olive oil
salt and freshly ground black pepper
2 tablespoons breadcrumbs
3 tablespoons finely chopped parsley
4 tablespoons dry white wine

Wipe and trim the mushrooms, then remove their stems and chop these finely. Mix the chopped stems with the shallots, garlic, spinach, thyme and egg. Moisten with a little of the olive oil and season to taste with salt and pepper. Sauté the mixture in a little more of the olive oil. Fill the mushroom caps with the mixture, sprinkle with the breadcrumbs and parsley. Pour the remaining oil and the white wine into a flameproof dish and heat through on the top of the cooker. Arrange the stuffed mushrooms in the dish and cook in a moderate oven (190 C, 375 F, gas 5) for 15–20 minutes.

Red cabbage with orange

450 g/1 lb red cabbage
2 small oranges
1 small onion
1 clove garlic, crushed
40 g/1$\frac{1}{2}$ oz caster sugar
2 tablespoons wine vinegar
salt and freshly ground black pepper
25 g/1 oz butter

Quarter the cabbage, remove the core then shred finely. Wash in cold salted water, drain and place in a large bowl. Grate the oranges and extract the juice. Add the onion, garlic, sugar, vinegar and salt and pepper to the cabbage with the rind and juice of the oranges. Leave overnight to marinate, tossing a few times. Melt the butter in a large saucepan or flameproof casserole then add the cabbage. Cover with a lid and simmer for 1$\frac{1}{4}$–1$\frac{1}{2}$ hours, stirring occasionally. When cooked the liquid should have evaporated.

Georgian vegetable rice

1 medium onion, chopped
100 g/4 oz green pepper, deseeded
    and chopped
4 tablespoons oil
225 g/8 oz rice
450 ml/$\frac{3}{4}$ pint stock or water
salt
1 tablespoon concentrated tomato
    purée
100 g/4 oz tomatoes, chopped

Fry the onion and pepper in the oil. Add the rice, fry briefly, then stir in the stock. Add salt to taste and the tomato purée. Bring to the boil, cover closely, then leave to simmer over a very low heat for 15–20 minutes until all the water is absorbed. Stir in the tomatoes just before serving.

Creamy marrow,
Marrow with paprika

Sweetcorn with cream sauce

Vegetable rice with spices

Peas with mushrooms

(Illustrated on page 147)

225 g/8 oz frozen or fresh peas
25 g/1 oz butter
100 g/4 oz button mushrooms
salt and freshly ground black pepper

Cook the peas for 3–5 minutes in boiling salted water. Drain. Melt the butter and fry the mushrooms until tender. Add the peas and season to taste with salt and pepper. Cook over a low heat, stirring gently until the peas are hot. Do not overcook. Serve with grilled meat or use as an omelette stuffing.

Peas with ham

(Illustrated on page 147)

50 g/2 oz butter
450 g/1 lb frozen or fresh peas
salt and freshly ground black pepper
pinch sugar (optional)
150 g/5 oz ham, chopped

Melt the butter in a saucepan, add the peas, salt and pepper to taste and sugar, if using. Allow the peas to heat through. Add the ham and cook gently a further 3–4 minutes. Stir gently so as not to break up the peas. Serve with chicken or veal dishes.

Mixed vegetables

Cut the cleaned vegetables into even-sized small pieces. Cook in a small quantity of boiling salted water until tender. Drain and finish as suggested below.

French-style

Briefly fry the cooked vegetables in butter, adding extra salt to taste. Suggested vegetables: carrots, peas, Brussels sprouts, French beans, spinach.

English-style

(Illustrated on page 146)

Turn the vegetables into a warmed serving dish and top with knobs of butter. Suggested vegetables: Brussels sprouts, cauliflower, cabbage, carrots, peas, runner beans.

Italian-style

(Illustrated on page 146)

Fry the vegetables briefly in olive oil, adding herbs of your choice such as oregano, basil, thyme, rosemary. Suggested vegetables: Brussels sprouts, courgettes, fennel, sweetcorn.

Polish-style

Turn the vegetables into a warmed serving dish and sprinkle with fried breadcrumbs. Suggested vegetables: beans, cauliflower, pumpkin, radish.

Ceylonese vegetable rice

100 g/4 oz carrots
100 g/4 oz leeks
50 g/2 oz butter
100 g/4 oz cabbage, shredded
100 g/4 oz cauliflower,
    broken into florets
50 g/2 oz frozen or fresh peas
generous pinch curry powder
salt and freshly ground black pepper
225 g/8 oz rice
300 ml/$\frac{1}{2}$ pint water

Cut the leeks and carrots into fine strips and fry in the butter for 3–4 minutes. Add the cabbage, cauliflower, peas, curry powder, salt and pepper to taste. Cook for 5 minutes, then add the rice and water. Place in a covered casserole dish and cook in a moderately hot oven (190 C, 375 F, gas 5) for 30 minutes.

Ratatouille

4 tablespoons olive oil
2–3 cloves garlic, crushed
2 large onions, coarsely chopped
675 g/$1\frac{1}{4}$ lb tomatoes,
    peeled and chopped
1 large aubergine, diced
450 g/1 lb courgettes,
    sliced thickly

1 large green pepper,
   deseeded and chopped
1 large red pepper,
   deseeded and chopped
salt and freshly ground black pepper

Heat the oil in a large frying pan and add the garlic and onion. Cook for 2–3 minutes before adding the tomatoes. Continue cooking for 5–10 minutes before adding the aubergine and courgettes. Cook until these are almost tender, then add the peppers and salt and pepper to taste. Cook until all the vegetables are tender, but not mushy — they should retain their shape and colour.

Courgettes provençale

450 g/1 lb young courgettes
225 g/8 oz tomatoes
3 tablespoons olive oil
1 medium onion, chopped
1 clove garlic, crushed
generous pinch dried rosemary
salt and freshly ground black pepper

Cut the courgettes into slices, having discarded the ends. Peel the tomatoes by placing them in a heatproof bowl and pouring over sufficient boiling water to cover. Leave for 1–2 minutes then make a slit in the tomato skins with a sharp knife: the skins should roll off easily. Chop the tomatoes coarsely.

Heat the olive oil in a large saucepan and add the onion and garlic. Cook over a moderate heat for 2–3 minutes before adding the courgettes. Cook for 5 minutes, then add the chopped tomatoes, the rosemary and seasoning to taste. Cook for a further 5–8 minutes, until the courgettes are tender.

Mixed vegetables English-style

Mixed vegetables Italian-style

Peas with ham,
Peas with mushrooms

Sauces

Garlic sauce

1 medium onion, chopped
50 g/2 oz butter
4–6 cloves garlic, crushed
50 g/2 oz plain flour
450 ml/¾ pint strong beef stock
salt
6 black peppercorns

Fry the chopped onion in the butter until golden brown. Stir in the garlic and cook for another minute. Stir in the flour, fry a little, then add the stock. Bring to the boil, stirring all the time. Add salt to taste and the peppercorns. Simmer for 10–15 minutes longer and strain before serving. Serve with beef or tongue.

Celeriac sauce

1 medium onion, chopped
75 g/3 oz butter
50 g/2 oz plain flour
450 ml/¾ pint beef or chicken stock
salt
6 black peppercorns
1 bay leaf
100 g/4 oz celeriac
1–2 teaspoons vinegar
pinch sugar
100 ml/4 fl oz single cream

Fry the chopped onion in the butter, stir in the flour, and fry for a few minutes. Add the stock, salt to taste, peppercorns and bay leaf and cook until the sauce thickens. Peel the celeriac and cut into very small dice. Cook in a small quantity of boiling water for about 15 minutes or until tender. Add a little vinegar and sugar just before the end of the cooking time. Strain the sauce, add the celeriac and re-heat gently. Remove from the heat and stir in the cream. This sauce goes well with chicken and other white meats.

Gherkin sauce

1 large carrot, diced
1 small onion, chopped
75 g/3 oz butter
50 g/2 oz plain flour
salt
6 black peppercorns
1 sprig thyme (optional)
1 bay leaf
600 ml/1 pint beef stock
100 g/4 oz large pickled gherkins
150 ml/¼ pint milk
150 ml/¼ pint single cream

Fry the carrot and onion in 50 g/2 oz of the butter. Stir in the flour, fry for a few minutes, add salt to taste and the peppercorns, thyme (if used), bay leaf and stock. Blend well, and bring to the boil. Reduce the heat to a gentle simmer. Peel the gherkins and add the peelings to the sauce. Simmer for 20–30 minutes until reduced by two-thirds. Add the milk, bring to the boil, remove from the heat and strain the sauce. Stir in the cream. Cut the peeled gherkins into dice, fry them lightly in the remaining butter and add to the sauce. Serve with grilled or barbecued steak or chops.

Gypsy sauce

75 g/3 oz streaky bacon, chopped
1 medium onion, chopped
3 cloves garlic, crushed
1 green pepper, deseeded and
  chopped
50 g/2 oz gherkins, chopped

75 g/3 oz mushrooms, chopped
salt
$\frac{1}{2}$–1 teaspoon paprika
1 tablespoon concentrated tomato
   purée
2 tomatoes, peeled and chopped

Fry the bacon until the fat runs, add the onion and cook until soft. Stir in the garlic, pepper, gherkins and mushrooms. Season with salt and paprika to taste, stir in the tomato purée and cook gently for 5–10 minutes. Add the tomatoes just before the end of the cooking time.

Spinach sauce

4 tablespoons mayonnaise
50 g/2 oz spinach purée
salt
pinch freshly grated nutmeg
2 tablespoons double cream

Beat the mayonnaise with the spinach purée and salt and nutmeg to taste. Fold in the cream. Serve with fish or hard-boiled or poached eggs.

Cold chive sauce

(Illustrated on page 150)

4 tablespoons mayonnaise
4 tablespoons natural yogurt
salt
lemon juice

2 tablespoons finely chopped chives
2 tablespoons double cream

Combine the mayonnaise with the yogurt and salt and lemon juice to taste. Fold in the finely chopped chives and the cream. This sauce goes well with fried or steamed vegetables.

Cold tomato sauce

(Illustrated on page 150)

4 tablespoons mayonnaise
1 tablespoon concentrated tomato
   purée
2 tablespoons natural yogurt
salt and white pepper
2 tablespoons double cream
2 medium tomatoes, peeled,
   deseeded and chopped

Combine the mayonnaise, tomato purée and yogurt with salt and pepper to taste and mix well. Fold in the cream and finely chopped tomatoes. Serve with cooked cauliflower, leeks, celery or asparagus.

Devilled sauce

(Illustrated on page 150)

4 tablespoons mayonnaise
2 tablespoons natural yogurt
2 tablespoons concentrated tomato
   purée
salt
paprika

1 green chilli, finely chopped
2 tablespoons double cream
Garnish (optional):
   1 radish, sliced
   1 leek, sliced
   1 tomato, cut into small wedges

Combine the mayonnaise, yogurt and tomato purée with salt and paprika to taste. Add the finely chopped chilli and fold in the cream. Garnish with the suggested vegetables, if desired.

Cheese sauce

40 g/1$\frac{1}{2}$ oz butter
40 g/1$\frac{1}{2}$ oz plain flour
salt and freshly ground white pepper
pinch ground mace
300 ml/$\frac{1}{2}$ pint milk or single cream
1 egg
2 egg yolks
75 g/3 oz well-flavoured cheese (e.g.
   mature Cheddar, Emmental),
   grated
Melt the butter and stir in the flour to make a smooth paste. Add the seasonings with the milk or cream and cook until the sauce thickens, stirring all the time. Cool slightly. Gradually beat in the egg, egg yolks, and grated cheese. If the sauce is not being used immediately, brush it with melted butter to prevent a skin forming. Use for vegetable gratin dishes, cauliflower cheese, etc.

◀

Cold sauces: Chive, Tomato, Devilled Parsley

Horseradish, Onion and Tomato sauces ▶

Cold sauces: Garlic, Beetroot, Tarragon ▶

Onion sauce

(Illustrated on page 151)

75 g/3 oz butter
225 g/8 oz onions, finely chopped
50 g/2 oz plain flour
salt
6 peppercorns
450 ml/1 pint beef stock
1 onion to garnish

Melt 50 g/2 oz of the butter and fry the onion until golden brown. Add the flour, salt, peppercorns and stock. Stir until the sauce thickens, then simmer for 1 hour. Slice the onion for the garnish into rings and fry in the remaining butter until golden. Strain the cooked sauce over the onions. Serve with beef or poached eggs.

Parsley sauce

(Illustrated on page 151)

75 g/3 oz butter
50 g/2 oz plain flour
250 ml/8 fl oz strong beef stock
250 ml/8 fl oz milk
salt and freshly ground black pepper
4 tablespoons chopped parsley
2 egg yolks
4 tablespoons double cream

Melt the butter and stir in the flour to make a smooth paste. Add the stock and milk with salt and pepper to taste and cook, stirring until the sauce thickens. Bring to the boil and remove from the heat. Add the finely chopped parsley and the egg yolks mixed with the cream. Heat through, but do not allow to boil. Serve with boiled ham or fish dishes.

Variation:
Chive sauce

Omit the parsley and add 4 tablespoons finely chopped chives in its place.

Horseradish sauce

(Illustrated on page 151)

75 g/3 oz butter
50 g/2 oz plain flour
salt and white pepper
pinch ground mace
450 ml/$\frac{3}{4}$ pint strong beef stock
100 ml/4 fl oz milk
75 g/3 oz fresh horseradish, grated, or creamed, bottled horseradish
40 g/1$\frac{1}{2}$ oz blanched almonds, chopped
100 ml/4 fl oz double cream

Melt the butter and stir in the flour over a very low heat to make a smooth paste. Add the salt, pepper, mace and stock and cook until the sauce thickens. Add the milk, simmer for a few minutes and remove from the heat. If using fresh horseradish blanch it for a few minutes in boiling water and drain well. Add the horseradish to the sauce with the almonds. Finally stir in the cream. Serve with roast beef.

Tomato sauce

(Illustrated on page 151)

1 large carrot, diced
1 small onion, chopped
50 g/2 oz butter
50 g/2 oz plain flour
salt
6 black peppercorns
1 bay leaf
225 g/8 oz ripe tomatoes, chopped
450 ml/$\frac{3}{4}$ pint strong beef stock
100 ml/4 fl oz red wine
1 tablespoon lemon juice
3 tablespoons soured cream

Fry the carrot and onion in the butter until soft. Stir in the flour and fry briefly. Add the salt, peppercorns, bay leaf, tomatoes and stock. Bring to the boil and simmer for 1 hour. Finally add the wine and lemon juice. Heat through, then rub the sauce through a sieve. Stir in the soured cream just before serving. Serve with pasta or rice dishes.

Cold garlic sauce

(Illustrated on page 151)

2 cloves garlic, crushed
250 ml/8 fl oz natural yogurt
salt and freshly ground white pepper
small bunch spring onions

Mix the garlic with the yogurt and season to taste with salt and pepper. Chill well. Just before serving slice the spring onions, including the green parts, and add to the sauce.

Cold tarragon sauce

(Illustrated on page 151)

250 ml/8 fl oz natural yogurt
2 tablespoons double cream
salt and freshly ground white pepper
2 tablespoons fresh chopped
  tarragon or 1 tablespoon dried
  tarragon

Combine the yogurt and cream and season to taste with salt and pepper. Stir in the tarragon and chill well. Serve with fish, eggs or cauliflower.

Cold beetroot sauce

(Illustrated on page 151)

50 g/2 oz cooked beetroot
250 ml/8 fl oz natural yogurt
2 tablespoons double cream
salt and freshly ground black pepper

Remove the skin from the beetroot and grate the beetroot finely into a bowl. Add the yogurt and cream

and season to taste with salt and pepper. Mix gently but thoroughly. Chill well before serving with cold beef, tongue or pork.

Hollandaise sauce

2 tablespoons white wine vinegar
2 large egg yolks
175 g/6 oz butter
salt and white pepper
lemon juice

Beat the vinegar with the egg yolks in a bowl or saucepan over a large saucepan of hot water until the sauce starts thickening. Gradually add cubes of the butter, letting each one melt before adding the next. Season with salt, pepper and lemon juice. Serve immediately; the sauce curdles quite easily so do not allow it to get too hot.

Leek sauce

1 large onion, finely chopped
75 g/3 oz butter
50 g/2 oz plain flour
450 ml/¾ pint strong beef stock
salt and freshly ground black pepper

2 medium leeks, washed and sliced
100 ml/4 fl oz double cream

Lightly fry the finely chopped onion in 50 g/2 oz of the butter. Stir in the flour and cook for 1–2 minutes. Add the stock and season to taste with salt and pepper. Bring to the boil and simmer for 1 hour. Sauté the leeks in the remaining butter until tender. Strain the sauce over the leeks and stir in the cream. Serve with roast beef or baked potatoes.

Cold horseradish sauce

2 tablespoons mayonnaise
4 tablespoons natural yogurt
pinch sugar
1–2 teaspoons lemon juice
salt
4 tablespoons double cream
25 g/1 oz fresh horseradish, grated,
  or creamed, bottled horseradish

Combine the mayonnaise with the yogurt, sugar, lemon juice and salt to taste. Lightly fold in the cream and finely grated horseradish. Serve with vegetable or potato croquettes or other fried vegetables.

Fennel salad with fruit, ▲
and with cucumber

◀

Carrot salad with walnuts,
grapefruit, apples, horseradish

Salads

Carrot and grapefruit salad

(Illustrated on pages 154–5)

225 g/8 oz carrots
1 large grapefruit
salt
pinch sugar (optional)
lemon wedges to garnish

Finely grate the carrots and peel and chop the grapefruit, removing all pith and membrane. Mix together the carrot and grapefruit and season with salt and sugar, if liked. Garnish with wedges of lemon.

Variation:
Carrot, grapefruit and cucumber salad

Dice 100 g/4 oz cucumber and add to the salad.

Carrot and walnut salad

(Illustrated on pages 154–5)

350 g/12 oz carrots
salt

pinch sugar (optional)
1–2 tablespoons lemon juice
16 walnut halves
50 g/2 oz raisins

Finely grate the carrots and season to taste with salt, sugar (if liked) and lemon juice. Toss well. Just before serving add the walnuts and raisins.

Variations:
Carrot and almond salad

Omit the walnuts and raisins and add 50 g/2 oz blanched, shredded almonds to the carrots.

Carrot and raisin salad

Omit the walnuts and increase the quantity of raisins to 100 g/4 oz.

Carrot and fig salad

Omit the walnuts and raisins and add 100 g/4 oz dried figs cut into strips.

Carrot salad with yogurt dressing

350 g/12 oz carrots
250 ml/8 fl oz natural yogurt

salt
1–2 tablespoons lemon juice
2 tablespoons chopped fresh dill or parsley

Finely grate the carrots. Season the yogurt with salt and lemon juice and stir in the dill or parsley. Pour over the carrots and mix well. Chill before serving.

Carrot salad with horseradish

(Illustrated on pages 154–5)

350 g/12 oz carrots
50 g/2 oz fresh horseradish, grated or creamed, bottled horseradish
75 g/3 oz prunes, stoned and soaked
salt
1–2 tablespoons lemon juice
pinch sugar (optional)

Finely grate the carrots and horseradish if using fresh. Chop the prunes, add to the carrot and horseradish and toss lightly. Add salt, lemon juice and sugar (if desired) to taste.

Carrot and apple salad

(Illustrated on pages 154–5)

2 medium dessert apples
3 tablespoons lemon juice
350 g/12 oz carrots
salt
1 teaspoon clear honey

Grate the apples and sprinkle with 1 tablespoon of the lemon juice. Grate the carrots and combine with the apple. Season to taste with salt. Mix together the honey and remaining lemon juice. Pour this dressing over the other ingredients and toss gently. Chill before serving.

Fennel salad with fruit

(Illustrated on page 155)

2 heads fennel
4 tablespoons oil
1–2 tablespoons lemon juice
salt and freshly ground black pepper
1 medium orange
1 medium grapefruit
1 medium dessert apple
40 g/1½ oz blanched almonds, chopped
Garnish:
    4 maraschino cherries
    4 slices orange

Finely slice the fennel. Mix together the oil and lemon juice and season to taste with salt and pepper. Pour over the fennel and leave to marinate for 20–30 minutes. Meanwhile peel and chop the fruit. Add the fruit and almonds to the fennel and mix well. Garnish each serving with a maraschino cherry and a slice of orange.

Fennel and cucumber salad

(Illustrated on page 155)

2 heads fennel
1 (75-g/3-oz) piece cucumber
1 medium carrot, diced
4 tablespoons oil
1 tablespoon lemon juice
salt and freshly ground black pepper
Garnish:
    4 black olives, stoned
    4 sprigs parsley

Cut the fennel and cucumber into strips. Add the diced carrot and mix well. Whisk the oil with the lemon juice and season to taste with salt and pepper. Pour the dressing over the salad and toss gently. Garnish each portion with an olive and a sprig of parsley.

Brussels sprouts and ham salad

(Illustrated on pages 158–9)

450 g/1 lb Brussels sprouts
1 onion, sliced
100 g/4 oz cooked ham, cut into strips
4 tablespoons oil
1 tablespoon wine vinegar
salt and freshly ground black pepper

Cook the Brussels sprouts in boiling salted water for 5–7 minutes, until just tender but not soft. Strain and rinse under the cold tap. Drain well, halve and place in a bowl with the onion and ham. Whisk the oil with the vinegar and season to taste with salt and pepper. Pour the dressing over the salad and toss gently.

Nettle and prune salad

(Illustrated on pages 158–9)

350 g/12 oz young nettle leaves or young spinach leaves
100 g/4 oz stoned prunes
75 g/3 oz shallots, chopped or 1 medium onion, chopped
100 ml/4 fl oz white wine
4 tablespoons olive oil
salt and freshly ground black pepper

Wash the nettle or spinach leaves and shake dry. Place in a bowl with the prunes and chopped shallots or onions. Whisk together the wine and oil and season to taste with salt and pepper. Just before serving, pour the dressing over the salad and toss gently.

Brussels sprouts and ham salad, ▶
Nettle and prune salad

Vegetable and smoked mackerel salad

157

Vegetable and smoked mackerel salad

(Illustrated on page 159)

1 medium smoked mackerel
½ onion, chopped
2 large tomatoes, cut into wedges
1 green pepper, deseeded and
  chopped
½ cucumber, cut into strips
2 tablespoons oil
1 tablespoon lemon juice
salt and freshly ground black pepper
1 hard-boiled egg, sliced, to garnish

Bone the mackerel and remove the skin, if preferred. Cut the flesh into pieces and place in a bowl with the onion, tomato, pepper and cucumber. Mix gently. Whisk the oil with the lemon juice and season to taste with salt and pepper. Pour the dressing over the salad and toss carefully. Garnish with slices of hard-boiled egg.

Pepper and tomato salad

450 g/1 lb red or green peppers
salt and freshly ground black pepper
1 small onion, chopped
2 tomatoes, cut into wedges
1 tablespoon concentrated tomato
  purée
4 tablespoons soured cream

Deseed the peppers and cut them into thin strips. Place them in a bowl, sprinkle with salt, cover and leave for 10–15 minutes. Pour off the excess juice. Add the onion and tomatoes. Mix the tomato purée with the soured cream and season with pepper. Pour the dressing over the salad and toss gently. Serve with grilled pork.

Pepper and egg salad

350 g/12 oz mixed red and green
  peppers, deseeded
2 hard-boiled eggs, chopped
50 g/2 oz cocktail onions
2 tablespoons double cream
2 tablespoons natural yogurt
salt
2–3 teaspoons lemon juice
pinch sugar (optional)

Cut the peppers into strips, put them into a sieve and pour over boiling water. Drain. Put them into a bowl, add the chopped hard-boiled eggs and cocktail onions. Mix together the cream and yogurt and season to taste with salt, lemon juice and sugar, if liked. Pour the dressing over the salad and toss gently. Chill well before serving.

Radish salad with soured cream

1 large bunch radishes
2 shallots, chopped
100 ml/4 fl oz soured cream
1 tablespoon chopped chives
salt and freshly ground black pepper

Slice the radishes and place in a bowl with the shallots. Mix together the soured cream and chives and season to taste with salt and pepper. Pour the dressing over the salad and toss gently. Chill well and serve with cold roast meat or use as a filling for peppers, tomatoes, etc.

Pepper and olive salad

450 g/1 lb mixed red and green
  peppers
1 large onion, sliced into rings
100 g/4 oz black olives, stoned
3 tablespoons oil
1 tablespoon vinegar
salt
2 teaspoons chopped fresh tarragon
  or 1 teaspoon dried tarragon

Core and deseed the peppers, then cut them into strips. Add the onion and olives. Toss lightly. Whisk together the oil and vinegar and season to taste with salt. Mix in the tarragon and pour the dressing over the salad. This goes well with lamb dishes.

Variation:

Pepper and onion salad

Omit the olives and use 2 large onions instead of 1. Use dill or parsley in place of the tarragon.

Radishes with spring onions

1 large bunch radishes
1 bunch spring onions
3 tablespoons oil
1 tablespoon lemon juice
salt and freshly ground black pepper

Slice the radishes and chop the spring onions. Place together in a serving dish. Whisk together the oil and lemon juice and season to taste with salt and pepper. Pour the dressing over the salad and toss well.

Spring onion salad
(Illustrated on page 162)

2 bunches spring onions
3-4 tablespoons olive oil
1 tablespoon wine vinegar
salt and freshly ground black pepper

Chop the spring onions, including the green parts, and place in a serving bowl. Whisk together the oil and vinegar and season to taste with salt and black pepper. Pour the dressing over and toss well.

Fennel salad with soy dressing
(Illustrated on page 163)

2 heads fennel
4 tablespoons oil
4 tablespoons soy sauce
salt and freshly ground black pepper
Garnish (optional):
    fresh fennel leaves
    1 tomato, peeled
    black olives
    1 onion, sliced
    piece cucumber, cut into strips

Cut the fennel into fine strips. Mix together the oil, soy sauce and salt and pepper to taste. Pour over the fennel and leave for 30 minutes for the flavour to develop before serving. Garnish with the suggested vegetables, if desired.

Chicory and ham salad

4 heads chicory
salt and freshly ground black p
1 dessert apple, cored and slic
1 tablespoon lemon juice
100 g/4 oz cooked ham,
    cut into strips
3 tablespoons double cream
3 tablespoons mayonnaise

Slice the chicory into strips, sprinkle with salt and set aside, covered, for 10 minutes. Sprinkle the apple slices with lemon juice to prevent discoloration. Pour the excess juice off the chicory and add the ham and apple. Season well with pepper. Mix together the cream and mayonnaise and stir into the salad. Serve with crusty French bread as a lunch or supper dish.

Blue cheese salad

225 g/8 oz tomatoes, chopped
225 g/8 oz red or green peppers,
    deseeded and chopped
225 g/8 oz cucumber, sliced
small bunch spring onions, chopped
small bunch radishes, sliced
3 tablespoons oil
1 tablespoon lemon juice
salt and freshly ground black pepper
100 g/4 oz blue cheese, diced

Place all the vegetables in a bowl and mix carefully. Whisk together the oil and lemon juice and season to taste with salt and pepper. Just before serving pour over the dressing and scatter over the cheese. Toss all the ingredients together gently.

Radish and cheese salad
(Illustrated on page 166)

2 bunches radishes
2 tablespoons oil
salt and freshly ground black pepper
75 g/3 oz Emmental or Cheddar
    cheese, grated

Slice the radishes, reserving a few for the garnish. Toss in the oil, salt and pepper. Top with the grated cheese. Garnish with radish roses. Serve with a cheese or cold meat platter.

Fennel salad with soy dressing

◀ *Spring onion salad*

Beetroot salad
with herb dressing

(Illustrated on page 166)

1 dessert apple
1 tablespoon lemon juice
225 g/8 oz cooked beetroot, diced
3 tablespoons natural yogurt
2 tablespoons mayonnaise
2 tablespoons double cream
2 shallots, finely chopped
50 g/2 oz gherkins, finely chopped
2 tablespoons chopped fresh herbs
   (e.g. parsley, chives, dill, tarragon,
   mint)
salt
dash Worcestershire sauce
Garnish (optional):
   chives
   2 button mushrooms, sliced
   gherkins

Peel and dice the apple and sprinkle with lemon juice to prevent discoloration. Mix the apple with the beetroot and place in a serving dish. Mix together the yogurt, mayonnaise and cream and stir in the shallots, gherkins and herbs. Season to taste with salt and Worcestershire sauce. Serve the sauce separately garnished with the chives, mushroom slices and gherkins, if using.

Celeriac and apple salad

350 g/12 oz celeriac
1 tablespoon tarragon or white wine
   vinegar

1 bay leaf
6 allspice berries
salt and freshly ground black pepper
350 g/12 oz dessert apples
3 tablespoons oil

Peel the celeriac and cut into thin strips. Just cover with boiling water and add the vinegar, bay leaf, allspice and salt and pepper to taste. Simmer for 5–10 minutes until just tender. Drain and cool, removing the bay leaf and spices. Just before serving peel and slice the apples and add to the celeriac. Toss in the oil gently and serve at once.

Lettuce and pickled
onion salad

(Illustrated on page 167)

1 lettuce
100 g/4 oz pickled onions, halved
3 tablespoons oil
1 tablespoon vinegar
salt and freshly ground black pepper

Wash and dry the lettuce, tear up the leaves and mix with the onions. Whisk the oil with the vinegar and season to taste with salt and pepper. Pour over the salad and toss gently.

Variation:
Lettuce and egg salad

(Illustrated on page 167)

Omit the pickled onions and toss the lettuce in the dressing. Slice

two hard-boiled eggs and arrange amongst the lettuce leaves.

Dandelion
and bacon salad

350 g/12 oz young dandelion leaves
   or young spinach leaves
225 g/8 oz streaky bacon, chopped
2 shallots, chopped
salt and freshly ground black pepper
1–2 teaspoons vinegar

Trim the dandelion or spinach, removing the tough stalks and wash well. Shake dry and place in a bowl. Fry the bacon until the fat runs, add the shallots and fry for a few minutes. Season with salt, pepper and vinegar to taste. Pour the hot bacon mixture over the dandelion or spinach and toss to coat. Serve at once as an accompaniment to roast or grilled meat.

Variation:
Dandelion salad
with paprika and cream

(Illustrated on page 166)

After frying the shallots add $\frac{1}{2}$–1 teaspoon paprika to the pan and cook for 1–2 minutes. Add 100 ml/4 fl oz soured cream, stir well and pour the hot dressing over the dandelion leaves.

Celeriac salad

450 g/1 lb celeriac
1 large onion, cut into wedges
4 tablespoons mayonnaise
3 tablespoons natural yogurt
salt
1–2 teaspoons lemon juice

Peel the celeriac and cut into thin strips. Just cover with boiling water and cook until tender (5–10 minutes). Add the onion and continue cooking until the onion is soft. Drain well. Combine the mayonnaise with the yogurt and season to taste with salt and lemon juice. Stir the dressing into the celeriac and onion. Allow to cool and chill well before serving.

Variation:
Celeriac and egg salad

Add 4 coarsely chopped hard-boiled eggs to the basic dressed salad.

Mixed salad with mushrooms

100 g/4 oz carrots, cut into strips
100 g/4 oz celeriac, cut into strips
225 g/8 oz cauliflower florets
100 g/4 oz button mushrooms, sliced
1 small onion, chopped
4 tablespoons oil

1 tablespoon lemon juice
salt and freshly ground black pepper

Place all the vegetables in a bowl and mix well. Whisk together the oil and lemon juice and season to taste with salt and pepper. Pour the dressing over the salad and toss gently.

Chicory and apple salad

4 heads chicory
salt and freshly ground black pepper
2 dessert apples, peeled, cored and finely grated
25 g/1 oz freshly grated horseradish or 50 g/2 oz grated radishes
3 tablespoons oil
1 tablespoon lemon juice

Cut the chicory into broad strips, put them into a bowl and sprinkle with salt. Put aside, covered, for 10 minutes, to eliminate the bitter taste. Pour off the juice and add the finely grated apples and horseradish or radish. Whisk together the oil and lemon juice and season to taste with salt and pepper. Pour the dressing over the salad and mix well.

Variations:
Chicory and carrot salad

Omit the apples and add 2 large coarsely grated carrots. Add 1 tablespoon chopped chives to the dressing.

Chicory and onion salad

Omit the apples and add 1 large finely chopped onion. Add 1 crushed garlic clove to the dressing.

Chicory and pepper salad

Omit the apples and add 1 large red pepper, deseeded and chopped.

Lettuce with lemon cream dressing

1 lettuce
100 ml/4 fl oz double cream
rind and juice of $\frac{1}{2}$ lemon
salt

Wash the lettuce and shake dry. Tear the leaves into pieces. Mix the cream with the lemon rind and juice and season to taste with salt. Toss the salad in the cream.

Variation:
Lettuce with soured cream dressing

Omit the double cream and lemon rind. Instead use 100 ml/4 fl oz soured cream and add 2 tablespoons chopped chives.

Beetroot salad with herb dressing

*Radish and cheese salad,
Dandelion salad with
paprika and cream*

*Lettuce and pickled onion
salad,
Lettuce and egg salad*

Asparagus and sweetcorn salad

225 g/8 oz cooked fresh asparagus
  or canned asparagus tips
225 g/8 oz canned young corn cobs
  or canned sweetcorn kernels
50 g/2 oz cocktail onions
3 tablespoons oil
1 tablespoon vinegar
salt and freshly ground black pepper

Cut the asparagus and corn cobs into even-sized pieces. If using canned vegetables drain well. Add the cocktail onions. Whisk the oil with the vinegar and season to taste with salt and pepper. Toss the vegetables in the dressing and chill well before serving.

Aubergine and ham salad

1 small onion, chopped
4 tablespoons oil
2 large aubergines, diced
225 g/8 oz cooked ham or smoked
  pork, diced
salt and freshly ground black pepper
2–3 teaspoons vinegar
2 teaspoons chopped fresh tarragon
  or 1 teaspoon dried tarragon

Fry the onion in the oil until beginning to soften. Add the aubergine and ham or smoked pork, cover the pan and cook gently until the aubergine is soft. Season well with salt and pepper. When

cool stir in vinegar to taste and the tarragon. Chill in the refrigerator before serving.

Celery and pea salad

1 head celery
225 g/8 oz cooked peas
2 tablespoons oil
1 tablespoon lemon juice
salt and freshly ground black pepper
1 tablespoon chopped chives

Wash the celery, trim and cut into strips. Add the peas. Whisk the oil with the lemon juice and season to taste with salt and pepper. Add the chives and pour the dressing over the salad. Toss gently.

Lettuce and fruit salad

1 lettuce
2 dessert apples
1 orange
2 tablespoons oil
1 tablespoon lemon juice
salt and freshly ground black pepper
50 g/2 oz walnuts or almonds,
  chopped, to garnish

Wash the lettuce, shake dry and tear the leaves into pieces. Peel and slice the apples and orange. Whisk the oil with the lemon juice and season to taste with salt and pepper. Garnish with the chopped

walnuts or almonds. Serve with veal or chicken.

Variation:
Lettuce and tropical fruit salad

Omit the apples and orange and use 2 tangerines or satsumas, divided into segments, 1 banana, thinly sliced, and 175 g/6 oz fresh pineapple, chopped. If liked, 4 tablespoons double cream may be added to the dressing.

Mixed pepper salad

1 red pepper, deseeded and sliced
1 green pepper, deseeded and sliced
25 g/1 oz mild chillies, chopped
100 g/4 oz tomatoes, cut into wedges
100 g/4 oz leeks, sliced
4 tablespoons oil
1 tablespoon vinegar
salt

Arrange the vegetables in a serving bowl. Whisk together the oil and vinegar and season to taste with salt. Pour the dressing over the salad and toss gently.

Lettuce and orange salad

2 heads lettuce
2 large oranges, peeled and chopped
4 tablespoons double cream

1–2 tablespoons lemon juice
salt

Wash the lettuce leaves and tear them into pieces, add the oranges and pour over the cream mixed with lemon juice and salt to taste. Toss lightly. Serve chilled.

Variation:

Lettuce and orange salad with egg

Omit the cream and use 100 ml/4 fl oz natural yogurt. Garnish the salad with 1 chopped hard-boiled egg.

Chicory salad with egg sauce

(Illustrated on page 171)

4 heads chicory
salt and freshly ground black pepper
3 tablespoons oil
2 egg yolks
1 teaspoon French mustard
juice of 1 lemon
1 teaspoon chopped parsley
tomato wedges to garnish

Slice the chicory and sprinkle with salt. Cover and put aside for 10 minutes. Drain off the juice. Blend the oil with the egg yolks, mustard, salt and pepper. Mix in the lemon juice. Sprinkle the chicory with parsley and garnish with tomatoes. Hand the sauce separately.

Vegetable and fruit crudités

(Illustrated on pages 170–1)

2 medium oranges
1 large grapefruit
2 dessert apples
1 tablespoon lemon juice
75 g/3 oz spring onions
75 g/3 oz prunes, stoned and halved
1 large or 2 medium carrots, sliced
75 g/3 oz pickled onions
4 small tomatoes, cut into wedges
75 g/3 oz cucumber, sliced
small bunch radishes, quartered
salt and freshly ground black pepper

Peel the oranges and grapefruit, removing all pith. Cut into slices. Peel and slice the apple and sprinkle with lemon juice to prevent discoloration. Arrange all the fruit and vegetables on a serving dish, season to taste and serve with cold tomato sauce (see page 149).

Vegetable salad with garlic sauce

100 g/4 oz tomatoes, sliced
100 g/4 oz cucumber, sliced
100 g/4 oz cooked ham, cut into strips
100 g/4 oz courgettes, sliced
1 large onion, sliced into rings
100 g/4 oz radishes, trimmed
1 large dessert apple, cored and sliced
1 tablespoon lemon juice

salt
small bunch spring onions, chopped
1 quantity cold garlic sauce
(page 152)

Arrange the vegetables on a glass platter. Sprinkle the apple slices with lemon juice and add to the vegetables. Sprinkle lightly with salt and chopped spring onions. Hand the cold garlic sauce separately.

Sweetcorn and ham salad

1 (397-g/14-oz) can miniature corn cobs
50 g/2 oz cooked ham, diced
50 g/2 oz red peppers, deseeded and sliced
50 g/2 oz pickled onions, chopped
3 tablespoons mayonnaise
3 tablespoons yogurt
salt and freshly ground black pepper
1–2 tablespoons lemon juice
1 teaspoon fresh thyme leaves or
1 tablespoon chopped parsley

Drain the corn cobs and place in a bowl with the ham, peppers, and onions. Mix the mayonnaise with the yogurt and season to taste with salt, pepper and lemon juice. Stir in the thyme or parsley. Toss the salad lightly in the dressing. Serve as a light cold supper.

◀ *Vegetable and fruit crudités*

Chicory salad with egg sauce
▼

Marinated cauliflower

1 medium cauliflower, broken into
   florets
1 large onion, sliced into rings
4 tablespoons oil
salt and freshly ground black pepper
1–2 tablespoons lemon juice
2 tablespoons chopped chives

Cook the cauliflower in boiling
water until just tender (5–10 minutes). Do not allow it to become
soft. Drain well and place in a dish
with a lid. Lightly fry the onion
in the oil and season well with salt
and pepper. Add lemon juice to
taste and stir in the chives. Pour
this dressing over the cauliflower.
Cover and leave in a cool place
overnight. Serve with veal or lamb,
or with a platter of cold meat.

Cucumber and tomato
salad with cream

½ cucumber, sliced
225 g/8 oz tomatoes, cut into wedges
100 ml/4 fl oz soured cream
3 tablespoons natural yogurt
salt and freshly ground black pepper
1–2 tablespoons lemon juice
1 tablespoon chopped chives

Place the cucumber and tomato
together in a bowl. Mix together
the soured cream and yogurt and
season generously with salt and

pepper. Add lemon juice to taste,
then fold in the chives. Pour the
dressing over the salad and chill
well before serving.

Pepper, tomato
and cucumber salad

1 large green pepper, deseeded and
   sliced into rings
225 g/8 oz tomatoes, sliced
100 g/4 oz cucumber, sliced
1 large onion, sliced into rings
3 tablespoons oil
1 tablespoon vinegar
salt and freshly ground black pepper
2 tablespoons chopped chives
100 g/4 oz Feta cheese

Layer the vegetables in a glass
bowl or arrange on a shallow platter.
Whisk together the oil and vinegar
and season well with salt and pepper.
Pour the dressing over the salad.
Sprinkle over the chives and finally
crumble over the Feta cheese.

Lettuce and tuna salad

1 medium lettuce, coarsely shredded
1 (198-g/7-oz) can tuna fish in oil
2 hard-boiled eggs, sliced
1 small onion, finely chopped
salt and freshly ground black pepper
lemon juice

Place the lettuce in a bowl. Flake
the tuna and add to the bowl with

the egg and onion. Toss gently.
Drizzle over a little of the oil from
the can of tuna and season to taste
with salt, pepper and lemon juice.

Cucumber salad
with green peppercorns

(Illustrated on page 174)

450 g/1 lb cucumber
2 tablespoons olive oil
2 tablespoons vinegar
salt
4 shallots, chopped
25 g/1 oz pickled green peppercorns

Slice the cucumber or cut in half
and slice lengthways using a potato
peeler or mandoline. Arrange in
a salad bowl. Mix the oil, vinegar
and salt together and pour over
the cucumber. Sprinkle with the
chopped shallots and green peppercorns. Serve with grilled meat.

Cucumber and
watermelon salad

(Illustrated on page 175)

1 large cucumber, peeled
juice of ½ lemon
salt
1 small watermelon

Scoop small balls out of the peeled
cucumber and marinate them for
10–15 minutes in the lemon juice

and salt. Scoop out balls from the watermelon pulp and mix with the marinated cucumber balls. Shape a basket out of the melon rind (see illustration) and turn the chilled salad into the basket. Alternatively dice the cucumber and melon flesh and serve in individual glass dishes.

Watercress salad with yogurt dressing

1 large bunch watercress, washed
50 g/2 oz finely chopped raw onion
4 tablespoons natural yogurt
2 tablespoons double cream
salt and freshly ground black pepper
1–2 tablespoons lemon juice

Place the watercress in a serving bowl. Mix the onion into the yogurt and fold in the double cream. Season with salt, pepper and lemon juice to taste. Pour the dressing over the salad. Serve with grilled pork chops.

Onion salad

450 g/1 lb onions
3 tablespoons olive oil
1 tablespoon vinegar
salt
$\frac{1}{2}$–1 teaspoon sugar

Slice the onions into rings. Whisk together the oil and vinegar. Sprinkle salt and sugar to taste over the

onions and pour over the dressing. Toss gently and leave to marinate for several hours.

Italian cucumber salad

1 large cucumber
2 tablespoons oil
2 egg yolks
salt and freshly ground black pepper
2–3 teaspoons lemon juice
$\frac{1}{2}$ teaspoon chopped parsley
50 g/2 oz cheese, grated

Slice the cucumber. Mix the oil, egg yolks, salt, pepper, lemon juice and chopped parsley to blend. Pour the dressing over the cucumber, add the grated cheese and stir. Serve chilled.

Cucumber and potato salad

225 g/8 oz cucumber
100 g/4 oz boiled potatoes, thickly sliced
150 ml/$\frac{1}{4}$ pint natural yogurt
2 tablespoons oil
1 tablespoon lemon juice
salt

Cut the cucumber into thick slices and place them in a bowl with the sliced potatoes. Blend together the yogurt, oil and lemon juice and add salt to taste. Serve with highly spiced dishes.

Cucumber salad with paprika dressing

1 large cucumber
3 tablespoons double cream
1–2 teaspoons lemon juice
salt
$\frac{1}{2}$ teaspoon paprika
1 tablespoon chopped parsley

Slice the cucumber. Mix the cream, lemon juice, salt, paprika and chopped parsley to make the dressing. Pour it over the cucumber and toss lightly. Serve chilled.

Cucumber and chilli salad

350 g/12 oz cucumber
50 g/2 oz mild chillies
4 tablespoons oil
1 tablespoon lemon juice
salt

Cut the cucumber into thin strips. Chop the chillies and add to the cucumber. Whisk together the oil and lemon juice and season with salt. Pour over the salad and toss gently.

Cucumber salad with green peppercorns ▶

Cucumber and watermelon salad

173

Mixed salad
with cream dressing

100 g/4 oz carrots, sliced
100 g/4 oz cucumber, sliced
100 g/4 oz tomatoes, sliced
1 bunch radishes, quartered
1 bunch spring onions, chopped
2 tablespoons oil
1 tablespoon lemon juice
1 tablespoon chopped dill or parsley
4 tablespoons double cream
salt and freshly ground black pepper

Put all the vegetables in a bowl and
mix together. Whisk together the
oil and lemon juice and stir in the
chopped dill or parsley and double
cream. Season to taste with salt and
pepper and pour over the salad.

Sauerkraut salad
with cranberries

(Illustrated on page 178)

350 g/12 oz canned or bottled sauer-
    kraut, rinsed
50 g/2 oz pickled onions, halved
2 tablespoons oil
salt
pinch sugar
100 g/4 oz bottled or tinned
    cranberries, drained

Cut the rinsed sauerkraut into small
pieces. Add the onions, oil, salt,
a pinch of sugar, and the drained
cranberries. Toss lightly and chill.
Serve with boiled beef or pork.

176

Onion and beetroot salad

450 g/1 lb onions, sliced into rings
100 g/4 oz cooked beetroot, grated
1 tablespoon vinegar
3 tablespoons water
pinch salt
pinch sugar
2 tablespoons oil

Mix the onion and beetroot together
in a bowl. Boil the vinegar with the
water, add the salt and sugar, then
pour the boiling liquid over the
onion and beetroot mixture. Leave
the salad in a cool place for a few
hours. Sprinkle with the oil before
serving.

Chilli salad
with lotus root

(Illustrated on pages 178-9)

225 g/8 oz fresh or dried lotus root
100 g/4 oz small chillies, sliced
50 g/2 oz spring onions, finely
    chopped
2 tablespoons oil
1 tablespoon lemon juice
salt
1-2 teaspoons curry powder

Thinly slice the fresh lotus root.
If using dried lotus root, soak in
hot water for 20 minutes, rinse,
then slice. Add the small chillies
and finely chopped onion, toss
lightly and pour over the oil, lemon

juice, salt and curry powder to
taste.

Chilli and
mushroom salad

(Illustrated on pages 178-9)

150 g/5 oz mild chillies
100 g/4 oz button mushrooms
100 g/4 oz young leeks
4 tablespoons oil
1 tablespoon vinegar
salt

Slice the chillies, mushrooms and
leeks, toss lightly and dress with
a mixture of the oil, vinegar and
salt.

Chilli and cheese salad

(Illustrated on pages 178-9)

100 g/4 oz mild chillies, sliced
1 large onion, sliced
100 g/4 oz hard cheese (e.g. Edam,
    Cheddar, Emmental), sliced
1 green pepper, deseeded and
    chopped
1 red pepper, deseeded and chopped
4 tablespoons oil
salt

Place the chillies, onion, cheese
and peppers together in a bowl
and mix together. Sprinkle over
the oil and season with salt to
taste. Serve with cold meat.

Chilli and bacon salad

225 g/8 oz mild chillies (green and red)
100 g/4 oz lean bacon
1 large onion
2 tablespoons oil
salt
vinegar

Halve and deseed the chillies. Cut the bacon and onion into strips, add the chillies, oil, salt and vinegar and toss lightly. Serve with boiled beef or pork.

Onion and apple salad

225 g/8 oz onions
350 g/12 oz apples, sliced
3 tablespoons mayonnaise
3 tablespoons double cream
3 tablespoons natural yogurt
salt and freshly ground white pepper

Slice the onions into rings and blanch in boiling salted water. Drain and cool. Add the apples and mix gently. Mix the mayonnaise, cream and yogurt together, then add salt and pepper to taste. Pour over the salad, toss lightly and chill.

Variation:
Onion and celeriac salad

Omit the apple and add 225 g/8 oz celeriac cut into thin strips to the

onion before blanching. Scatter 25 g/1 oz chopped walnuts over the top just before serving.

Red cabbage and apple salad

350 g/12 oz red cabbage, shredded
225 g/8 oz dessert apples, cored and sliced
2 tablespoons oil
1 tablespoon vinegar
salt

Place the cabbage and apples together in a bowl. Whisk together the oil and vinegar and season to taste with salt. Pour the dressing over the salad and toss gently. Serve with roast pork.

Variation:
Red cabbage and grape salad

Omit the apple and use 225 g/8 oz black grapes, halved and deseeded. Alternatively use 100 g/4 oz grapes and 100 g/4 oz apple.

Onion and mushroom salad

350 g/12 oz onions, sliced into rings
dash vinegar
225 g/8 oz mushrooms, sliced

4 tablespoons oil
salt and freshly ground black pepper
1–2 tablespoons lemon juice
1 tablespoon chopped chives

Blanch the onions in boiling water to which a dash of vinegar has been added. Fry the mushrooms lightly in the oil and season to taste with salt, pepper and lemon juice. Cool and mix with the onions. Sprinkle with chives and chill before serving.

Variation:
Onion and pepper salad

Omit the mushrooms and use 2 medium green peppers, deseeded and cut into strips.

Tomato and mushroom salad

450 g/1 lb tomatoes, peeled and quartered
225 g/8 oz button mushrooms, sliced
1 small onion, chopped
2 tablespoons oil
salt and freshly ground black pepper

Combine the tomatoes, mushrooms and onion in a bowl. Pour over the oil and season to taste with salt and pepper. Toss gently.

Sauerkraut salad with cranberries ▶
Chilli and cheese salad, Chilli and bacon salad, Chilli salad with lotus root, Chilli and mushroom salad

177

Broccoli salad
with capers

450 g/1 lb broccoli, broken into
    florets
50 g/2 oz capers
75 g/3 oz pickled onions
3 tablespoons oil
1 tablespoon smooth prepared
    mustard
1 tablespoon lemon juice
salt and freshly ground black pepper

Cook the broccoli in boiling salted water until just tender. Drain and cool. Place in a bowl with the capers and pickled onions. Mix together the oil, mustard and lemon juice. Season to taste with salt and pepper. Pour the dressing over the salad and toss gently.

Onion and carrot salad

450 g/1 lb onions
225 g/8 oz carrots
3 tablespoons oil
1 tablespoon wine vinegar
1 teaspoon lemon juice
salt and freshly ground black pepper
1 teaspoon sugar

Halve the onions and cut into rings. Place in a colander or sieve and blanch by pouring a kettle of boiling water over them. Drain and cool. Add the carrots, cut into strips, and toss lightly. Mix the oil, vinegar, lemon juice, salt, pepper and sugar together and pour over the salad, toss again and chill. Serve with roast or grilled meat.

Sauerkraut salad
with carrots and honey

(Illustrated on page 182)

450 g/1 lb canned or bottled sauer-
    kraut, rinsed
100 g/4 oz carrots, grated
3 tablespoons honey
salt

Cut the rinsed sauerkraut into small pieces. Add the grated carrots and honey. Season to taste with salt, stir and chill. Serve with cold roast meat.

Sauerkraut
and bean salad

(Illustrated on page 182)

350 g/12 oz canned or bottled sauer-
    kraut, rinsed
100 g/4 oz canned borlotti or red
    kidney beans, drained
1 small onion, finely chopped
3 tablespoons oil
salt and freshly ground black pepper
1–2 tablespoons lemon juice

Press the sauerkraut to remove the excess juice. Put it into a bowl with the beans, finely chopped onion and oil. Season to taste with salt, pepper and lemon juice. Stir and chill well. Serve with boiled or stewed beef.

Variations:
Sauerkraut and
mushroom salad

Omit the beans and add 100 g/4 oz sliced button mushrooms to the salad.

Sauerkraut
and pickled onion salad

Omit the beans and add 100 g/4 oz halved pickled onions and 50 g/2 oz cooked ham cut into strips.

Oriental salad

(Illustrated on page 183)

225 g/8 oz fresh or dried lotus root,
    sliced
1 avocado, peeled and chopped
100 g/4 oz mild chillies
4 tablespoons oil
1 tablespoon lemon juice
generous pinch each salt, curry
    powder, coriander, cinnamon

If using dried lotus root soak for 20 minutes in hot water, then rinse before using. Mix the vegetables together in a bowl. Whisk together the oil and lemon juice and season with salt. Mix in the spices. Pour the dressing over the salad. Stir to coat and leave in a cool place for a few hours before serving to allow the flavours to blend.

Spinach and radish salad

350 g/12 oz young spinach leaves
100 g/4 oz pickled onions
small bunch radishes, sliced
3 tablespoons oil
1 tablespoon wine vinegar
salt and freshly ground black pepper

Wash the spinach and remove the stalks. Cut the leaves into broad strips and put into a bowl together with the pickled onions and radishes. Whisk the oil with the vinegar and season to taste with salt and pepper. Pour the dressing over the salad and toss gently.

Aubergine and olive salad

675 g/1½ lb aubergines
1 medium onion, coarsely chopped
4 tablespoons oil
salt and freshly ground black pepper
1–2 tablespoons lemon juice
2 tablespoons chopped dill or parsley
12 stuffed, green olives, sliced

Peel the aubergines, if desired, halve lengthways and slice thinly. Lightly fry the onion in the oil. Add the aubergine and salt and pepper to taste and cook gently until tender. Cool and season with lemon juice and stir in the dill or parsley. Fold in the olives. Chill well before serving. Serve with a cold roast or smoked pork.

Cabbage with yogurt dressing

350 g/12 oz white cabbage, shredded
100 g/4 oz button mushrooms, sliced
1 large onion, chopped
150 ml/¼ pint natural yogurt
2–3 teaspoons lemon juice
salt and freshly ground black pepper
2 tablespoons chopped dill or parsley

Place the cabbage, mushroom and onion together in a bowl. Season the yogurt to taste with lemon juice, salt and pepper, then fold in the chopped dill or parsley. Pour the dressing over the salad and mix gently.

Cabbage and apple salad

(Illustrated on page 195)

350 g/12 oz white cabbage, shredded
225 g/8 oz dessert apples
100 g/4 oz pickled onions
3 tablespoons oil
1 tablespoon lemon juice
salt

Place the shredded cabbage in a serving dish. Reserve half an apple for the garnish and peel and finely slice the remainder. Add to the cabbage with the pickled onions. Whisk together the oil and lemon juice and season to taste with salt. Pour the dressing over the salad and toss gently. Just before serving slice the remaining apple and use to garnish the salad.

Beetroot and potato salad

225 g/8 oz cooked beetroot, diced
225 g/8 oz boiled potatoes, diced
1 large onion, chopped
225 g/8 oz cucumber, chopped
3 tablespoons oil
1 tablespoon vinegar
salt and freshly ground black pepper
1 tablespoon chopped dill or parsley

Place the vegetables together in a bowl. Whisk together the oil and vinegar and season to taste with salt and pepper. Stir in the dill or parsley. Pour the dressing over the salad and toss gently.

Tomato and olive salad

450 g/1 lb tomatoes, sliced
50 g/2 oz black olives, stoned and halved
50 g/2 oz pickled onions, halved
2 tablespoons olive oil
1 tablespoon lemon juice
salt and freshly ground black pepper
2 teaspoons chopped fresh tarragon or 1 teaspoon dried tarragon

Arrange the tomatoes, olives and onions on a serving dish. Whisk together the oil and lemon juice and season to taste with salt and pepper. Stir in the tarragon. Pour the dressing over the salad. Serve with a cold meat or cheese platter.

▲
Sauerkraut and bean salad,
Sauerkraut and pickled onion salad,
Sauerkraut and mushroom salad,
Sauerkraut salad with carrots
and honey

Oriental salad ▶

Leek and spring onion salad

350 g/12 oz leeks, sliced
1 bunch spring onions, chopped
3 tablespoons oil
1 tablespoon lemon juice
salt and freshly ground black pepper

Blanch the leeks for 1 minute in boiling water. Drain and cool. Place in a bowl and scatter over the spring onions. Whisk together the oil and lemon juice and season to taste with salt and pepper. Pour the dressing over the salad and toss gently.

Variation:

Leek and mushroom salad

Omit the spring onions and use 100 g/4 oz sliced button mushrooms.

Cauliflower and meat salad

1 cauliflower
2 tablespoons mayonnaise
2 tablespoons natural yogurt
2 tablespoons double cream
1 tablespoon chopped chives
salt and freshly ground black pepper
1 tablespoon lemon juice

175 g/6 oz roast meat (e.g. beef, lamb, pork), diced

Divide the cauliflower into florets and cook in boiling water until just tender. Mix the mayonnaise, yogurt, cream and finely chopped chives in a deep bowl. Season to taste with salt, pepper and lemon juice. Add the cooled cauliflower and the meat. Toss gently and chill well. Serve as a light cold supper or use as a filling for peppers or tomatoes.

Tomato and egg salad

450 g/1 lb tomatoes
3 tablespoons oil
1 tablespoon lemon juice
salt and freshly ground black pepper
1 tablespoon finely chopped chives
2 hard-boiled eggs, sliced

Slice the tomatoes and arrange them on a platter. Mix the oil with the lemon juice, salt, pepper and finely chopped chives. Pour the dressing over the tomatoes and top with slices of hard-boiled egg.

Tomato salad with yogurt dressing

450 g/1 lb tomatoes
2 tablespoons chopped chives
100 ml/4 fl oz natural yogurt
1–2 tablespoons lemon juice
salt and freshly ground black pepper

Slice the tomatoes and arrange on a serving dish. Fold the chives into the yogurt and add lemon juice to taste. Season well with salt and pepper, then chill thoroughly. Pour the dressing over the tomatoes just before serving.

Variation:

Tomato salad with dill dressing

Omit the chives and add 2 tablespoons chopped dill to the dressing. If you like 2 tablespoons double cream may be added to the yogurt for a creamier flavour.

Chinese cabbage salad

(Illustrated on page 186)

350 g/12 oz cabbage
5 small dried chillies
3 tablespoons oil
25 g/1 oz Chinese mushrooms, soaked in hot water for 10 minutes and chopped
50 g/2 oz canned pimiento, cut into strips
1–2 teaspoons vinegar
salt
1 tablespoon soy sauce
pinch ground ginger
1 leek to garnish (optional)

Cut the cabbage into squares, blanch in boiling water and drain. Fry the chillies on all sides in the oil, remove them from the pan and pour the oil over the cabbage. Add the Chinese mushrooms and the pimiento. Season with the vinegar, salt, soy sauce and ginger to taste. Finely slice the leek, if using, and sprinkle over the salad.

Red cabbage salad with cream dressing

(Illustrated on page 187)

350 g/12 oz red cabbage
1 small onion, finely chopped
4 tablespoons soured cream
salt and freshly ground black pepper
lemon juice
Garnish (optional):
  1 onion
  1 tomato

Finely shred the cabbage and place in a bowl. Mix together the onion and soured cream and season to taste with salt, pepper and lemon juice. Mix the dressing into the cabbage, or hand separately if preferred. To make the garnish peel and halve the onion, then push out the layers to make cups. Cut the edge of each cup in a zig-zag pattern and place a piece of tomato in the centre.

Cabbage salad with fruit

(Illustrated on page 186)

350 g/12 oz white cabbage
50 g/2 oz prunes, stoned and soaked

50 g/2 oz dried apricots, soaked
50 g/2 oz raisins
50 g/2 oz seedless grapes
3 tablespoons oil
1 tablespoon lemon juice
salt and freshly ground black pepper
1 dessert apple, sliced, to garnish

Finely shred the cabbage and chop the prunes and apricots. Mix together in a bowl and add the raisins and grapes. Whisk together the oil and lemon juice and season to taste with salt and pepper. Pour the dressing over the salad. Garnish with slices of apple.

Tomato salad with basil

5 tomatoes
1 bunch shallots or spring onions, finely chopped
4 tablespoons finely chopped basil
3 tablespoons finely chopped tarragon
3 tablespoons finely chopped parsley
3 tablespoons olive oil
1 tablespoon white wine vinegar
1 teaspoon prepared mustard
salt and freshly ground black pepper

Cut the tomatoes into wedges and sprinkle over the shallots or spring onions. Mix the finely chopped herbs together and sprinkle over the tomatoes. Whisk together the oil, vinegar, mustard and salt and pepper to taste. Pour the dressing over the tomatoes, onions and herbs.

Savoy cabbage salad

1 small Savoy cabbage
1 onion
5 tablespoons white wine vinegar
3 tablespoons oil
generous pinch caster sugar
salt and white pepper
75 g/3 oz mixed nuts
  (e.g. blanched almonds,
  hazelnuts, cashews)

Shred the cabbage into fine strips, removing the hard stalk. Blanch the strips in boiling salted water for 5 minutes then drain. Finely dice the onion. Make a dressing from the wine vinegar, oil, caster sugar, salt and pepper. Add the diced onion and pour over the cabbage. Mix together well, then toss in the nuts just before serving.

Chinese cabbage salad

Cabbage salad with fruit

*Red cabbage salad
with cream dressing* ▶

Celery stuffed with cream cheese

225 g/8 oz cream or curd cheese
2 tablespoons double cream
1 tablespoon brandy
pinch celery salt
1 teaspoon paprika
generous pinch white pepper
generous pinch ground ginger
4 sticks celery
2 small gherkins to garnish
　(optional)

Mix the cream or curd cheese with the double cream, brandy, celery salt, paprika, pepper and ground ginger and blend together well. Trim the sticks of celery into 7.5-cm/3-in lengths and place or pipe the cheese mixture into the celery. Slice the gherkins (if desired) and use to garnish the celery rolls. Chill before serving.

Chicory, tomato and walnut salad

3 heads chicory
450 g/1 lb tomatoes
50 g/2 oz walnuts, finely chopped
4 tablespoons oil
2 tablespoons white wine vinegar
1 clove garlic, crushed
salt and freshly ground black pepper
1 tablespoon chopped parsley to
· garnish (optional)

Cut the chicory heads in half and slice each half finely. Arrange the slices in the middle of a plate. Slice the tomatoes and place around the edge of the plate. Sprinkle the finely chopped walnuts over the chicory in the centre of the plate. Whisk together the oil, vinegar, garlic, salt and pepper to taste and pour over the salad. Sprinkle the parsley over the top, if using.

Fennel salad with yogurt

1 large fennel
1 cucumber, diced
6 radishes, sliced
1 head chicory
1 large grapefruit
6 tablespoons natural yogurt
1 tablespoon chopped mint
salt and freshly ground white pepper

Finely slice the fennel and mix with the diced cucumber and sliced radish. Slice the chicory and add to the salad. Cut the grapefruit in half and take out the segments and add these to the salad. Mix the yogurt and mint together, add salt and pepper to taste, then pour over the salad ingredients.

Celery and apple salad

1 head celery
2 dessert apples
juice $\frac{1}{2}$ lemon
50 g/2 oz walnuts, chopped

Cut the celery into small slices. Core the apples and slice thinly, then sprinkle with the lemon juice to prevent discoloration. Mix the celery and apple together with the walnuts.

Spinach salad

225 g/8 oz young, fresh spinach
3 stick celery, sliced
2 large tomatoes, sliced
12 black olives, stoned
4 tablespoons olive oil
2 tablespoons white wine vinegar
salt and freshly ground black pepper
75 g/3 oz pine nuts

Wash the spinach thoroughly, drain well and chop. Mix the drained, chopped spinach with the celery slices, sliced tomato and olives. Whisk together the oil, vinegar, and salt and pepper to taste, then pour over the salad. Sprinkle the pine nuts on top and serve.

Onion and orange salad

(Illustrated on pages 190–1)

225 g/8 oz oranges
225 g/8 oz onions, sliced into rings
2 tablespoons honey
2 tablespoons oil
1 tablespoon lemon juice
salt

Thinly pare the rind from one of

the oranges and reserve for the garnish. Peel the oranges, removing all trace of pith, and slice thinly. Arrange in a serving dish with the onion. Whisk together the honey, oil and lemon juice and season to taste with salt. Pour the dressing over the salad. Cut the reserved orange peel into thin strips and blanch for 2 minutes in boiling water, then drain, cool and scatter over the salad.

Leek and chilli salad

(Illustrated on page 191)

225 g/8 oz leeks
100 g/4 oz mild chillies
2 tablespoons oil
1 tablespoon wine vinegar
salt

Finely slice the leeks, blanch in boiling water for 1 minute and drain. Cool and add the chillies. Whisk together the oil and vinegar and season to taste with salt. Pour the dressing over the salad and chill well before serving. This salad goes well with pork dishes.

Cabbage and orange salad

(Illustrated on page 191)

350 g/12 oz white cabbage, shredded
1 large orange or 2 satsumas, divided
   into segments

50 g/2 oz blanched almonds
2 tablespoons oil
1 tablespoon lemon juice
salt

Place the cabbage, orange and almonds together in a bowl. Whisk together the oil and lemon juice and season to taste with salt. Pour the dressing over the salad and toss gently.

Variation:

Cabbage and pineapple salad

Omit the orange or satsumas and use 175 g/6 oz chopped fresh pineapple or pineapple pieces canned in their own juice.

Asparagus and egg salad

350 g/12 oz fresh or canned
   asparagus
4 small tomatoes
4 hard-boiled eggs
5 tablespoons oil
3 tablespoons white wine vinegar
salt and freshly ground white pepper

If using fresh asparagus boil or steam in a little salted water until tender. Drain the canned asparagus, if using. Finely dice the peeled and deseeded tomatoes. Cut the eggs into eight wedges and arrange on a flat dish with the tomatoes and

asparagus cut into 2.5-cm/1-in pieces. Whisk together the oil, vinegar and salt and pepper to taste and pour this dressing over the salad.

Mushroom and prawn salad

350 g/12 oz mushrooms
100 g/4 oz peeled prawns,
   defrosted if frozen
3 tablespoons oil
1 tablespoon white wine vinegar
1 teaspoon lemon juice
salt and freshly ground white pepper
1 tablespoon finely chopped chives
   to garnish

Clean and trim the mushrooms and cut into thin slices. Mix the prawns with the mushrooms. Whisk together the oil, vinegar, lemon juice and salt and pepper to taste. Pour this dressing over the mushrooms and prawns and garnish with the finely chopped chives.

Onion and orange salad ▶
Leek and chilli salad,
Cabbage and orange salad

Mixed pepper salad

3 large peppers, red, green and
  yellow
1 onion
3 tablespoons white wine vinegar
8 tablespoons oil
2 teaspoons chopped mixed herbs
salt and freshly ground white pepper

Core and deseed the peppers, then
cut into very thin slices. Cut the
onion also into thin slices. Whisk
together the wine vinegar, oil, herbs
and salt and pepper to taste. Pour
the dressing over the mixed peppers
and onion rings.

Potato and gherkin salad

450 g/1 lb new potatoes
6 tablespoons mayonnaise
  (page 201)
4 pickled gherkins, sliced
salt and freshly ground white pepper

Boil the new potatoes in their
jackets until tender. Leave to cool
slightly, then cut into small pieces.
Mix in the mayonnaise and gherkins,
then add salt and pepper to taste.
Chill before serving.

Potato and celery salad

450 g/1 lb potatoes
8 tablespoons mayonnaise
  (page 201)

2 teaspoons finely chopped onion
2 sticks celery, sliced
salt and freshly ground white pepper
1 tablespoon chopped parsley to
  garnish (optional)

Cook the potatoes in boiling salted
water until just tender. Drain and
leave to cool slightly, then cut
into cubes. Mix in the mayonnaise,
onion, celery, salt and pepper to
taste. Chill before serving sprinkled
with the parsley, if wished.

Vegetable
and fruit cocktail

(Illustrated on page 194)

lettuce
tomatoes
bananas
apples
celeriac
oranges
walnuts
oil
lemon juice
salt and freshly ground black pepper

This cocktail should be served at
a cold buffet or garden party. The
quantity of the ingredients depends
on the number of people to be
served and on the size of the glass
bowl. Cut all the vegetables and
fruit into cubes or slices. Arrange
them attractively in the glass bowl.
Mix oil and lemon juice together
in proportions 3 : 1. Season to taste

with salt and pepper and pour the
dressing over the salad just before
serving. Garnish with halved walnuts.

Beetroot and apple salad
with walnuts

(Illustrated on page 195)

225 g/8 oz dessert apples
225 g/8 oz cooked beetroot, diced
1–2 tablespoons lemon juice
salt and freshly ground black pepper
1 teaspoon fennel seeds (optional)
75 g/3 oz walnut halves

Reserve half an apple for the garnish. Peel, core and dice the remainder and place in a bowl with
the beetroot. Sprinkle with lemon
juice and season with salt, pepper
and fennel seeds, if using. Add the
walnuts and garnish with slices of
the remaining apple.

Cucumber and
prawn salad

1 cucumber
225 g/8 oz peeled cooked prawns,
  defrosted if frozen
3 tablespoons oil
1 tablespoon white wine vinegar
$\frac{1}{2}$ teaspoon grated lemon rind
generous pinch sugar
salt and freshly ground white pepper

Cut the cucumber in half lengthways and remove the seeds with a teaspoon. Slice the cucumber halves very finely. Mix the cucumber with the prawns in a salad bowl. Beat the oil with the vinegar, lemon rind, sugar and season to taste with salt and pepper. Stir this dressing into the cucumber salad and leave for 30–60 minutes before serving.

Mushroom salad

450 g/1 lb mushrooms
100 g/4 oz smoked ham
3 tablespoons oil
2 teaspoons white wine vinegar
2 teaspoons lemon juice
pinch sugar
1 tablespoon sherry
salt and freshly ground pepper

Clean and trim the mushrooms and cut into very thin slices. Cut the smoked ham into thin strips or dice. Mix the mushrooms and ham together in a salad bowl. Beat the oil with the vinegar, lemon juice, sugar, sherry and season to taste with salt and pepper. Pour this dressing over the mushroom salad. Cover and chill for 30 minutes before serving.

Broccoli and mushroom salad

450 g/1 lb young broccoli
9 tablespoons oil

1 tablespoon white wine vinegar
3 tablespoons dry sherry
salt and freshly ground pepper
1 egg yolk
1 teaspoon mild prepared mustard
½ teaspoon mustard powder
1½ tablespoons lemon juice
dash Worcestershire sauce
100 g/4 oz mushrooms

Trim the broccoli, cutting off any leaves or thick stalks. Blanch the broccoli in boiling water for 3 minutes, then drain and leave to cool. Beat together 3 tablespoons of the oil with the vinegar, sherry and seasoning to taste. Separate the broccoli into small florets, put in a bowl and pour over the dressing. Cover and leave to stand for 30–60 minutes.

Beat the egg yolk with the mustard, mustard powder, 1 tablespoon lemon juice and the Worcestershire sauce. Gradually whisk in the remaining oil, a little at a time, until the mixture becomes creamy. Trim and thinly slice the mushrooms and sprinkle with the remaining lemon juice. Arrange the broccoli and mushrooms on a flat dish and serve the mayonnaise separately.

Chicory and orange salad

4 small heads chicory
2–3 oranges
3 tablespoons oil
1 tablespoon lime juice
1 teaspoon sugar

generous pinch ground ginger
½ teaspoon prepared mustard
freshly ground black pepper

Trim the chicory and separate the leaves. Peel the oranges, removing all the pith, and separate into segments. Discard any pips and skin. Beat the oil with the lime juice, sugar, ground ginger, mustard and pepper to taste. Pour this dressing over the chicory and orange in a salad bowl and toss well.

Celery and carrot salad

4 carrots
2 sticks celery
½ lemon
pinch sugar
3 tablespoons double cream
salt and freshly ground black pepper

Grate the carrots into long strips. Slice the celery sticks very finely. Place the carrot and celery, mixed together, into a salad bowl. Pour over the lemon juice and sprinkle over the sugar. Toss the salad lightly. Beat the cream with a generous amount of salt and pepper to taste. Pour the cream over the salad and mix in just before serving.

Vegetable and fruit cocktail

194

Cabbage and apple salad, Beetroot and apple salad with walnuts

Dressings, marinades, vinegars and flavoured butters

Vegetable and wine marinade

50 g/2 oz carrots
50 g/2 oz celeriac
50 g/2 oz shallots
50 g/2 oz leeks
150 ml/$\frac{1}{4}$ pint white wine
4 tablespoons oil
salt and freshly ground black pepper

Cut the vegetables into thin strips and cook gently in the wine until tender. Add a little extra water, if necessary, during cooking. Cool and add the oil. Season to taste with salt and pepper.

Oriental vegetable marinade

(Illustrated on page 198)

50 g/2 oz carrots
50 g/2 oz celeriac
50 g/2 oz onion
50 g/2 oz green peppers
50 g/2 oz button mushrooms
2 tablespoons oil
4 tablespoons white wine
salt and freshly ground black pepper

2 tablespoons concentrated tomato purée
1 tablespoon soy sauce

Cut all the vegetables into strips and fry briefly in the oil. Add the wine and salt and pepper to taste, then simmer gently until just tender. Add the tomato purée and soy sauce and stir gently. Remove from the heat and allow to cool.

Vegetable curry marinade

(Illustrated on page 198)

3 tablespoons mayonnaise
3 tablespoons natural yogurt
3 tablespoons double cream
1 teaspoon lemon juice
pinch salt
1 teaspoon curry powder
50 g/2 oz fresh or dried lotus root or 175 g/6 oz cooked potatoes, sliced
2–4 mild chillies
50 g/2 oz cocktail onions
1 hard-boiled egg yolk

Mix the mayonnaise, yogurt, cream, lemon juice, salt and curry powder together in a deep bowl. If using dried lotus root soak for 20 minutes

in hot water first. Add the sliced lotus root or potatoes, onions, chillies and decorate with grated egg yolk.

Dill and vegetable dressing

(Illustrated on page 198)

50 g/2 oz cucumber, diced or scooped into balls
50 g/2 oz cooked celeriac, diced
50 g/2 oz cooked carrots, diced
100 ml/4 fl oz natural yogurt
2 tablespoons double cream
salt and freshly ground black pepper
1–2 tablespoons lemon juice
2 tablespoons chopped dill or parsley

Place the vegetables together in a bowl. Mix together the yogurt and cream and season to taste with salt, pepper and lemon juice. Stir in the dill or parsley. Pour the dressing over the vegetables and mix gently.

Pepper vinegar

(Illustrated on page 199)

350 g/12 oz red or green peppers
1 litre/1$\frac{3}{4}$ pints wine vinegar

Remove the core and seeds from the peppers and cut them into thin strips. Place them in a wide-necked screw-top glass jar or a Kilner jar. Add the wine vinegar, cover and leave for 7–10 days. Pass through a fine sieve and store in smaller bottles.

Lemon vinegar

(Illustrated on page 199)

rind and juice of 4 lemons
1 litre/1¾ pints wine vinegar

Use a sharp knife or potato peeler to pare the rind from the lemons. Cut the rind into thin strips and place in a wide-necked, screw-top jar or Kilner jar. Add the lemon juice and vinegar. Cover the bottle and leave for 6–8 days. Pass the vinegar through a fine sieve and store in smaller bottles in a cool and dark place. Make orange vinegar in the same way.

Carnation-scented vinegar

(Illustrated on page 199)

2–3 handfuls of small fragrant
    carnations
1 litre/1¾ pints wine vinegar

Cut off the stems and remove the bracts from the carnations. Leave them to dry slightly in an airy place. Put them into a wide-necked, screw-

top jar or Kilner jar and add the vinegar. Close the bottle and leave the vinegar for 15 days. Pass the vinegar through a filter into smaller bottles and store in a cool and dark place.

Violet-scented vinegar

(Illustrated on page 199)

2–3 handfuls violets
1 litre/1¾ pints wine vinegar

Cut off the leaves and stems of the violets and leave the flowers to dry a little in an airy place. Put them into a wide-necked, screw-top jar or Kilner jar and add the vinegar. Cover and leave in a warm, sunny place for 14 days. Pass the vinegar through a fine sieve into smaller bottles. Store in a cool, dark place.

Tarragon and shallot vinegar

175–225 g/6–8 oz fresh tarragon
    leaves
4–5 bay leaves
5–6 cloves
150 g/5 oz shallots, coarsely chopped
1 litre/1¾ pints wine vinegar

Leave the tarragon leaves to dry slightly in a warm, airy place. Put them into a wide-necked bottle, screw-top jar or Kilner jar and add the spices and shallots. Pour

over the vinegar. Cover the bottle and leave for 14 to 16 days. Pass the vinegar through a fine sieve and store in smaller bottles.

Tarragon vinegar

(Illustrated on page 199)

75–100 g/3–4 oz fresh tarragon
1 litre/1¾ pints wine vinegar

Leave the tarragon to dry slightly in a dry, airy place. Put it into a wide-necked bottle, screw-top jar or Kilner jar and add the vinegar. Cover and leave for 14–16 days. Pass the vinegar through a fine sieve and store in smaller bottles.

Shallot vinegar

(Illustrated on page 199)

100–150 g/4–5 oz shallots, coarsely
    chopped
1 litre/1¾ pints wine vinegar

Place the shallots in a wide-necked, screw-top jar or Kilner jar and add the vinegar. Close the bottle and leave for 14–20 days. Pass the vinegar through a fine sieve and store in smaller bottles.

Marinades: Dill and vegetable dressing, Vegetable curry, Vegetable and wine, Oriental vegetable

Vinegars: Lemon, Violet-scented, Carnation-scented, Pepper, Herb, Tarragon, Tarragon and shallot, Shallot

Herb vinegar

50 g/2 oz fresh basil
50 g/2 oz garlic
25 g/1 oz fresh bay leaves
1 litre/1¾ pints wine vinegar

Leave the basil, garlic and bay leaves to dry a little. Chop them finely, put into a wide-necked, screw-top jar or a Kilner jar and add the vinegar. Cover and leave for 3–4 weeks. Pass the vinegar through a fine sieve and store in smaller bottles.

Garlic butter

100 g/4 oz butter
3 cloves garlic, crushed
salt

Cream the butter and beat with the salt and finely sliced or crushed garlic. Wrap the butter in foil and chill until firm. Slice off portions as required.

Shallot butter

100 g/4 oz butter
salt and freshly ground black pepper
1 tablespoon smooth prepared mustard
2–3 teaspoons lemon juice
4 shallots, very finely chopped

Cream the butter and beat in the salt, pepper, mustard, lemon juice and finely chopped shallots. Blend and chill. Use the butter to season mild-tasting vegetable dishes.

Horseradish cream

(Illustrated on page 23)

50 g/2 oz fresh horseradish
½ teaspoon prepared mustard
1 teaspoon white wine vinegar
salt
pinch sugar
300 ml/½ pint double cream, whipped

Finely grate the horseradish, add the wine vinegar, mustard, salt and a pinch of sugar. Fold in the whipped cream. Serve with smoked or roast meat, grilled fish, etc.

Horseradish and apple relish

(Illustrated on page 23)

100 g/4 oz fresh horseradish, finely grated
225 g/8 oz dessert apples, grated
salt and freshly ground black pepper
pinch sugar
1–2 tablespoons lemon juice or vinegar

Mix the grated horseradish and apples together. Season to taste with salt, pepper, sugar and lemon juice or vinegar. Stir to mix and chill before serving.

Horseradish and beetroot relish

(Illustrated on page 23)

100 g/4 oz fresh horseradish
225 g/8 oz pickled beetroot, diced or grated
pinch sugar
salt
1–2 tablespoons lemon juice

Finely grate the horseradish and mix with the beetroot. Season to taste with sugar, salt and lemon juice. Serve with roast, boiled or smoked meat.

Egg-yolk dressing

1 tablespoon prepared mustard
3 tablespoons oil
2 yolks from hard-boiled eggs, sieved
salt and freshly ground black pepper
1 tablespoon lemon juice
1 tablespoon chopped parsley

Beat the mustard with the oil in a deep bowl until smooth. Stir in the egg yolks, salt and pepper to taste, lemon juice and parsley.

Herb dressing

8 tablespoons olive oil

3 tablespoons white wine vinegar
1 tablespoon finely chopped, mixed
  tarragon and chives
pinch salt and freshly ground black
  pepper

Mix all the ingredients together in a screw-topped jar and shake well to combine.

Herb butter

100 g/4 oz butter
2 shallots, very finely chopped
25 g/1 oz gherkins, very finely
  chopped
5 capers, chopped
2 anchovy fillets, mashed (optional)
2 tablespoons chopped, fresh mixed
  herbs
salt and freshly ground black pepper

Cream the butter and beat in all the other ingredients. Form into a roll, wrap in foil or greaseproof paper and chill until hard. Slice off portions as required.

Mayonnaise

2 egg yolks
pinch mustard powder
salt and freshly ground white pepper
pinch caster sugar (optional)
300 ml/$\frac{1}{2}$ pint oil
1–2 tablespoons white wine vinegar
  or lemon juice

Place the egg yolks, mustard powder, salt and white pepper and sugar (if using) in a blender or liquidizer. Begin the machine and gradually pour in the oil. When thick add the wine vinegar or lemon juice to thin the mixture down to the required consistency. Taste and adjust the seasoning as necessary.

Paprika butter

$\frac{1}{2}$ teaspoon concentrated tomato
  purée
pinch cayenne
generous pinch caster sugar
100 g/4 oz butter, softened
1 tablespoon paprika

Mix together the tomato purée, cayenne and sugar with the softened butter and blend thoroughly. Spread the butter on aluminium foil or greaseproof paper to a thickness of 1 cm/$\frac{1}{2}$ in and chill. Cut into rectangles or squares and coat in the paprika.

Maître d'Hôtel butter

100 g/4 oz butter
2 tablespoons chopped parsley
1 tablespoon lemon juice
$\frac{1}{2}$ teaspoon salt
generous pinch cayenne

Cream the butter until it has softened and is smooth. Beat in the parsley and lemon juice, then add the salt and cayenne. Mix in well and adjust the seasoning, if necessary.

Courgette and fruit cups

German pancakes with rhubarb

Fried marrow with cinnamon ▶

Desserts

Courgette and fruit cups

(Illustrated on page 202)

225 g/8 oz quark or cottage cheese
2 tablespoons redcurrant jelly
225 g/8 oz courgettes, thinly sliced
3 tablespoons double cream
225 g/8 oz fresh fruit (apple, orange,
    grapefruit, redcurrants, etc.)
For decoration:
    lemon slices
    grated carrot
    walnut halves
    prunes

Mix together the quark or cottage cheese, jelly, courgettes and cream. Fill sundae glasses with this mixture and top with fruit as suggested. Decorate as desired.

Fried marrow with cinnamon

(Illustrated on page 203)

675 g/1½ lb marrow
100 ml/4 fl oz milk
2 eggs
50 g/2 oz plain flour

1 tablespoon caster sugar
oil for frying
50 g/2 oz icing sugar
1 teaspoon cinnamon

Peel and halve the marrow. Remove the seeds and cut into 1-cm/½-in slices. Make a batter out of the milk, eggs, flour and caster sugar. Dip the marrow slices in the batter and shallow fry in oil until golden brown. Drain and dip in the icing sugar. Arrange on a serving plate and sprinkle with cinnamon. Serve with whipped cream and fresh fruit.

Carrot biscuits

150 g/5 oz plain flour
75 g/3 oz butter or block margerine
    at room temperature
1 egg yolk
75 g/3 oz carrots, finely grated
caster sugar or icing sugar for
    sprinkling

Sieve the flour into a bowl, rub in the fat until the mixture resembles fine breadcrumbs, then add the egg yolk and carrots. Work together with the hands to make

a smooth dough. Roll out the dough quite thinly and cut out various shapes. Bake in a moderately hot oven (190 C, 375 F, gas 5) for 25–30 minutes. Sprinkle the caster or icing sugar over the biscuits while still hot.

German pancakes with rhubarb

(Illustrated on pages 202 and 207)

400 g/14 oz cottage cheese or quark
75 g/3 oz fine semolina
2 eggs
40 g/1½ oz sugar
pinch salt
oil for frying
300 ml/½ pint double or soured
    cream
450 g/1 lb stewed rhubarb or pumpkin

Sieve the cottage cheese if using this. Mix the cottage cheese or quark with the semolina, eggs, sugar and salt to make a dough. Form into small, flat pancakes and fry on both sides in the oil until golden brown. Serve hot topped with the double or soured cream and pieces of rhubarb or pumpkin.

Carrot cream with nuts

225 g/8 oz cream cheese
225 g/8 oz carrots, finely grated
pinch salt
1–2 tablespoons lemon juice
1–2 tablespoons sugar
100 ml/4 fl oz double cream
10 walnuts, halved

Mix the cream cheese with the carrots and salt. Season to taste with lemon juice and sugar. Stir in the double cream. Pile the mixture into individual glass dishes and garnish with the walnuts.

Courgettes filled with fruit

(Illustrated on page 206)

2 medium courgettes
100 g/4 oz cream cheese or quark
2 tablespoons double cream
40 g/1½ oz fruit purée (e.g. apricot, redcurrant)
Garnish:
    100 g/4 oz fruit (e.g. banana, orange, redcurrant, pineapple, etc.)
    walnut halves

Cut the courgettes into various shapes such as tiny barrels, and partially scoop out the flesh. Fill with the cream cheese or quark beaten with the cream and puréed fruit. Garnish with the fruit and a walnut half.

Carrot and nut soufflé

50 g/2 oz butter
50 g/2 oz plain flour
150 ml/¼ pint single cream
½ teaspoon ground cinnamon
2 tablespoons fresh white breadcrumbs
4 eggs, separated
225 g/8 oz carrots, finely grated
225 g/8 oz dessert apples, peeled and grated
butter for greasing the dish
40 g/1½ oz walnuts, chopped

Melt the butter and stir in the flour to make a smooth paste. Add the cream and cinnamon. Cook until the sauce thickens. Cool slightly, then add the breadcrumbs, egg yolks, carrots and apples. Whisk the egg whites until stiff but not dry, then fold into the mixture. Pour into an ovenproof dish greased with the butter. Sprinkle over the chopped walnuts and bake in a moderately hot oven (200 C, 400 F, gas 6) for 1 hour until well risen and golden brown.

Candied cucumber

675 g/1½ lb cucumber
225 g/8 oz sugar
100 ml/4 fl oz white wine
3 tablespoons water
thinly pared rind and juice of ½ lemon
1 (2.5-cm/1-in) piece cinnamon stick
3–4 cloves

Peel and quarter the cucumbers, then remove the seeds. Cut the quarters into pieces about 4 cm/1½ in long. Blanch in boiling water for 2 minutes. Drain and arrange in a china or glass bowl. Put the sugar, white wine and water in a saucepan and heat gently until the sugar is completely dissolved. Add the lemon rind and juice and cinnamon stick, then boil for 10 minutes. Pour the syrup over the cucumber and marinate in the refrigerator for 3–4 days.

Apricots with carrots

350 g/12 oz carrots
1 (410-g/14½-oz) can apricots
1 tablespoon lemon juice
1 tablespoon sugar
4 tablespoons whipped cream

Finely grate the carrots. Add the apricots cut into small pieces and stir lightly. Add a little of the apricot juice, lemon juice and the sugar. Spoon the mixture into glass bowls. Chill well before serving, topped with the cream.

*Courgettes filled
with fruit*

Carrot pizza

Cottage cheese dumplings with rhubarb

German pancakes with rhubarb

Carrot pizza

(Illustrated on page 206)

Dough:
150 ml/¼ pint milk
1 teaspoon caster sugar
15 g/½ oz dried yeast
200 g/9 oz strong plain flour
pinch salt
40 g/1½ oz butter
1 egg yolk
Filling:
2 medium carrots
1 dessert apple
50 g/2 oz digestive biscuits, crushed
rind of 1 lemon, grated
25 g/1 oz sugar
2 eggs, beaten
2 tablespoons double cream
50 g/2 oz sultanas
1 egg yolk for brushing
1 tablespoon icing sugar for
    sprinkling

First make the dough. Warm the milk to blood heat and stir in the caster sugar. Sprinkle over the yeast and leave in a warm place for about 10 minutes or until frothy. Meanwhile sieve the flour and salt into a bowl and rub in the butter. Make a well in the centre and pour in the yeast mixture and egg yolk. Mix to combine the ingredients, then turn out onto a floured board and knead until smooth and elastic. Cover with oiled polythene and leave in a warm place until doubled in size. Turn out of the bowl, knead briefly, then press with the hands to form a circle on an oiled baking sheet.

Now make the filling. Grate the carrots and apple, add the crushed biscuits, grated lemon rind, sugar, eggs and cream. Mix lightly. Spread the filling on the dough to within about 1 cm/½ in of the edge. Scatter over the sultanas and brush the edge of the dough with egg yolk. Bake in a moderately hot oven (200 C, 400 F, gas 6) for 20–25 minutes or until golden brown. Sprinkle with icing sugar and serve warm.

Cottage cheese dumplings with rhubarb

(Illustrated on page 207)

2 stale white rolls
2 tablespoons milk
350 g/12 oz cottage cheese, sieved,
    or quark
225 g/8 oz fine semolina
pinch salt
2 eggs, beaten
40 g/1½ oz butter, melted
2 tablespoons caster sugar
450 g/1 lb rhubarb, stewed with
    sugar to taste, to serve

Remove the crust from the rolls and cut them into small dice. Soak in the milk and add the cottage cheese or quark, semolina and a pinch of salt, then the eggs. Mix to a smooth dough. Form small dumplings. Cook them in boiling water for 5–7 minutes, drain and drizzle over a little melted butter and sprinkle with sugar. Serve hot with stewed rhubarb.

Carrot whip

2 egg whites
50 g/2 oz caster sugar
225 g/8 oz carrots, finely grated
juice of 1 orange
juice of ½ lemon
40 g/1½ oz flaked almonds

Whisk the egg whites until they form stiff peaks. Fold in the sugar, carrots and orange and lemon juice. Serve at once sprinkled with the almonds.

Carrot squares

675 g/1½ lb carrots
75 g/3 oz butter
100 g/4 oz caster sugar
100 ml/4 fl oz single cream
100 g/4 oz walnuts, finely chopped
40 g/1½ oz icing sugar

Cook the carrots in slightly salted water until tender, then allow to cool. Finely grate the carrots and mix them with 50 g/2 oz of the butter, the caster sugar and cream. Cook the mixture in a saucepan over a medium heat until a thick purée is formed. Grease a small baking tin with the remaining butter and turn the carrot mixture into the tin. Bake in a moderate oven (180 C, 350 F, gas 4) for 30–40 minutes. Cut into squares while still warm and dip them into a mixture of the finely chopped walnuts and the icing sugar.

Carrot and potato pudding

75 g/3 oz finely grated potato
75 g/3 oz finely grated carrot
$\frac{1}{2}$ teaspoon bicarbonate of soda
50 g/2 oz sultanas
50 g/2 oz raisins
50 g/2 oz currants
50 g/2 oz brown sugar
50 g/2 oz caster sugar
50 g/2 oz flour
pinch salt
1 teaspoon baking powder
1 teaspoon ground ginger
25 g/1 oz butter, softened

Mix together the potato, carrot and bicarbonate of soda. Just cover the dried fruit with hot water and leave to soak for 5 minutes. Place the sugars, flour, salt, baking powder and ground ginger into a large bowl. Drain the fruit and add this and the potato and carrot mixture to the bowl. Add the softened butter and beat in until well mixed. Turn into a greased 600-ml/1-pint pudding basin and cover first with a circle of greased greaseproof paper and then with a circle of foil which has been pleated in the middle to allow the pudding to rise. Tie securely with string. Place the basin in a large saucepan half filled with boiling water and steam for 2 hours. Add more boiling water to the pan as necessary to keep the water level at halfway.

Carrot flip

Iced courgette cup

Tomato cocktail

Drinks

Carrot flip
(Illustrated on page 210)

250 ml/8 fl oz carrot juice
  (see below)
300 ml/$\frac{1}{2}$ pint single cream
4 egg yolks
100 ml/4 fl oz fresh orange juice
crushed ice
freshly grated nutmeg to garnish

Put the carrot juice, cream, egg yolks and orange juice into a cocktail shaker and mix well. Alternatively place in a bowl and whisk to combine thoroughly. Pour into glasses containing crushed ice and garnish with a little grated nutmeg.

Iced courgette cup
(Illustrated on page 210)

225 g/8 oz courgettes
juice of 1 lemon
50 g/2 oz sugar
4 tablespoons Maraschino liqueur
  or brandy
600 ml/1 pint sparkling white wine,
  chilled
crushed ice

Thinly slice the courgettes. Put them into a large glass bowl, sprinkle with the lemon juice and sugar, add the Maraschino or brandy and leave in a cool place for 1 hour. Add the sparkling wine and crushed ice just before serving.

Carrot juice

450 g/1 lb carrots, finely grated
50 g/2 oz sugar
juice of 1 lemon
600 ml/1 pint water

Sprinkle the carrots with the sugar and lemon juice, and leave in a cool place for a few minutes. Add the cold water and leave to stand for 1 hour. Pass through a sieve. Serve the juice as it is or use as a basis for other drinks.

Iced cucumber cup

225 g/8 oz cucumber
50 g/2 oz fresh root ginger, coarsely
  sliced
150 g/5 oz sugar

4 tablespoons Cointreau or another
  orange liqueur
750 ml/1$\frac{1}{4}$ pints white wine, chilled
750 ml/1$\frac{1}{4}$ pints sparkling white wine,
  chilled

Peel the cucumber, slice thinly and put into a large glass bowl. Add the coarsely sliced ginger, sugar and Cointreau, and chill for 2 hours. Remove and discard the ginger and add the wine and sparkling wine just before serving.

Tomato cocktail
(Illustrated on page 211)

450 g/1 lb tomatoes
1 large grapefruit
2 egg yolks
100 ml/4 fl oz double cream
salt and freshly ground black pepper
Garnish:
  freshly grated nutmeg

Immerse the tomatoes briefly in boiling water and slip off the skins. Chop roughly and place in a blender or liquidizer. Peel the grapefruit and divide into segments. Add these to the tomatoes with the egg yolks, cream and salt and pepper to taste. Blend well and pass through a sieve.

212

Garnish with a little freshly grated nutmeg.

Variation:
Tomato cooler
(*Illustrated on page 214*)

Omit the egg yolks and cream and add a generous quantity of crushed ice to the strained juice. Serve in tall glasses.

Courgette cooler
(*Illustrated on page 214*)

225 g/8 oz courgettes
4 tablespoons vodka
juice of 1 lemon
crushed ice
300 ml/½ pint tonic water
lemon and courgette slices to garnish

Roughly chop the courgettes. Put the vodka, lemon juice, ice and courgettes into a blender or liquidizer and liquidize until smooth. Strain into glasses and top up with tonic water. Garnish with a slice of lemon and a slice of courgette.

Rhubarb cup

450 ml/1 pint rhubarb, chopped
50 g/2 oz sugar
300 ml/½ pint water
juice of 1 lemon
2 slices fresh or canned pineapple, chopped

300 ml/½ pint orange juice
soda water (optional)

Place the rhubarb in a saucepan with the sugar, water and lemon juice. Bring to the boil and simmer for 5–10 minutes until tender. Cool and transfer into a large glass bowl, add the chopped pineapple, orange juice and top up with soda water, if desired.

Cucumber and apple cup

225 g/8 oz cucumber
rind of 1 lemon
juice of 2 lemons
50 g/2 oz sugar
600 ml/1 pint sparkling apple juice
300 ml/½ pint soda water

Peel and dice the cucumber. Place into a large glass bowl, add the lemon rind (if possible pared in one piece) and juice from 2 lemons, sprinkle with the sugar and leave in a cool place for 2–3 hours. Add the apple juice and soda water just before serving.

Tomato ginger cream
(*Illustrated on page 215*)

600 ml/1 pint tomato juice
250 ml/8 fl oz soured cream
ground ginger
4 slices lemon to garnish

Whisk the tomato juice with the soured cream. Pour into four glasses and sprinkle a generous pinch of ground ginger over each one. Garnish with slices of lemon.

Carrot milk shake
(*Illustrated on page 214*)

300 ml/½ pint carrot juice (see page 212)
300 ml/½ pint milk or half milk, half cream
honey
grated rind of 1 orange

Whisk together the carrot juice, milk and honey to taste. Pour into glasses and garnish with grated orange rind.

Rhubarb milk shake
(*Illustrated on page 214*)

225 g/8 oz stewed rhubarb
600 ml/1 pint milk
honey
Garnish (optional):
    orange wedges
    4 strawberries

Blend the milk with the rhubarb and honey to taste. Pour into glasses and garnish with wedges of orange and strawberries, if desired.

Tomato and courgette coolers

Carrot and rhubarb milk shakes

Tomato ginger cream ▶

Storing and preserving vegetables

The vitamin and biological values, taste and look of vegetable dishes depend not only on the culinary preparation but above all on the quality of the vegetables. Although fresh vegetables are the most valuable, correct storing can minimize the loss of nutritional substances and taste.

Short-term storing

Vegetables can be stored for a short period either in a refrigerator, or in a cool place, e.g. larder. The optimum temperature is 1–3 C/33 –37 F. The lowest temperature should never drop below zero, because the vegetables lose their taste and consistency, and the vitamin content decreases. Salad vegetables and spinach are damaged by light, which destroys their colour and vitamins. The light also accelerates evaporation and the vegetables tend to wither. They should be kept in dishes covered with a damp tea-towel or aluminium foil. The bottom of the dish can be sprinkled with a little crushed ice.

Long-term storing

A cool cellar is the best place for long-term storing. The vegetables must be undamaged, unbroken and unaffected by disease. Never wash the vegetables before storing, as humidity enhances moulding and spreading of rot-inducing bacteria. Store the vegetables on airy wooden trays.

Bottling

It is unfortunately not possible to bottle vegetables as they do not contain sufficient acid to stop bacterial action which will lead to fermentation and possibly food poisoning. Rhubarb is the only exception to this: technically a vegetable it is regarded by many as a fruit and does indeed contain a large percentage of acid.

The fruit to be bottled should be packed as tightly as possible into jars scalded with boiling water. Boiling syrup — composed of 225 g/8 oz sugar to 600 ml/1 pint water (though the amount of sugar can be varied according to the sweetness required) — should be added until it covers the fruit. Fasten the top on lightly and place the jars in a large saucepan of warm water, bring to simmering point — 88 C/190 F — which should take about 25–30 minutes and maintain this temperature there for 2 minutes. Remove the jars from the water and fasten the lids on tightly. Leave for 24 hours, then test that a seal has been made by removing the screw bands or clip tops and holding the jar by the lid only. If the lid remains securely in position then a vacuum has been successfully created.

An alternative method of sterilization is to place the jars — without screws or clip tops on the lid — on a baking sheet lined with folded newspaper. Put into a cool oven (150 C, 300 F, gas 2) for 30–40 minutes, then proceed as above.

Stewed rhubarb

(Illustrated on page 218)

1 kg/2¼ lb rhubarb
450 g/1 lb sugar
1 lemon, sliced
6 cloves
2 sticks cinnamon

Cut the rhubarb into 2.5-cm/1-in pieces. Place in a saucepan and sprinkle with the sugar. Heat gently until the juice runs from the rhubarb. Remove from the heat and cool. Put the rhubarb into jars scalded with boiling water and add a few thin slices of lemon, the cloves and a piece of cinnamon stick. Add enough sugar syrup to cover the fruit, close the bottles and sterilize as above.

Rhubarb in wine

(Illustrated on page 218)

1 kg/$2\frac{1}{4}$ lb rhubarb
675 g/$1\frac{1}{2}$ lb sugar
100 ml/4 fl oz white or red wine
juice of 1 lemon
1 cinnamon stick
1 (2.5–cm/1–in) piece fresh root
   ginger, bruised
6 cloves

Cut the rhubarb into 2.5–cm/1–in pieces. Mix them with the sugar and leave in a glass or china bowl set in a cool place for 1 day. Pour off the juice and place in a saucepan. Add the wine, lemon juice and spices and bring to the boil. Transfer the rhubarb into bottles, add the juice and close the bottles. Sterilize as above.

Freezing

It is probably true to say that freezing has become the most popular method of preserving and storing vegetables. Only good quality, young and tender vegetables should be used and then most vegetables should keep well for up to a year. It is essential to blanch most vegetables before freezing: this means immersing the prepared vegetables — washed, peeled and/or trimmed as normally done before cooking — in a large saucepan of rapidly boiling water. Remove from the water and chill quickly in cold running water or a large bowl of iced water. Drain thoroughly, dry on kitchen paper or a tea-towel, then pack in polythene bags or containers and freeze.

Artichokes, Globe — Cut off stalk. Trim point from each leaf. Wash well and remove choke by scraping it out with a teaspoon. Add a tablespoon of lemon juice to the water and blanch immediately, to prevent discoloration, for 7 minutes.

Asparagus — Rinse well and cut off woody base of spears. Scrape white part of stem downwards to remove scales. Blanch for 2 minutes for thin spears, 4 minutes for thick.

Aubergine — Wipe and then trim both ends. Dice or slice, then blanch for 4 minutes.

Beans — Top, tail and string the beans, then cut as required. Blanch for 2 minutes.

Beetroot — Trim off leaves and wash. Using only very small beetroot cook completely, slip off skins and leave whole.

Broccoli — Wash well and trim off coarse leaves and any very thick stems. Soak in salted water for 30 minutes, rinse and blanch for 3–5 minutes depending on size.

Brussels sprouts — Wash, trim off outer leaves and cut a cross in the base of large sprouts. Blanch for 3–4 minutes.

Cabbage — Remove coarse outer leaves, shred and blanch for 2 minutes.

Carrots — Top, tail, peel or scrape. Slice or dice, then blanch for 3 minutes.

Cauliflower — Wash well, divide into florets and blanch for 3 minutes.

Celeriac — Wash, peel, then slice or dice. Blanch for 3 minutes.

Courgettes — Wash, trim both ends and slice or cut into sticks. Blanch for 2 minutes.

Mushrooms — Wipe well, then freeze without blanching.

Parsnips — Trim both ends, peel and cut into slices or dice. Blanch for 2 minutes.

Peas — Shell and blanch for 1 minute.

Stewed rhubarb, Rhubarb in wine ▶
Growing vegetables at home

Peppers — Wash, halve or slice — removing seeds, core etc. Blanch for 2–3 minutes.

Pumpkin — Wash, peel and cut into chunky pieces, discarding seeds and pith. Cook completely in boiling salted water for about 30 minutes, then mash and freeze.

Spinach — Wash very thoroughly and blanch leaves for 2 minutes.

Swede — Trim off stalk and root ends. Peel and dice, then blanch for 5 minutes.

Sweetcorn — Strip husks and silks off cobs. Wash and either strip niblets off with a sharp knife and blanch for 2 minutes or leave whole and blanch for 4–5 minutes.

Turnips — Trim stalks and tapering root. Peel and dice. Blanch for 3 minutes.

Sauerkraut

5 kg/11 lb cabbage
100 g/4 oz salt
15 g/$\frac{1}{2}$ oz caraway seeds
100 g/4 oz onions

Remove the stalks and finely shred the cabbage. Mix with the salt, caraway and sliced onions. Pack into glass, wooden or earthenware vessels. To press out all the air and so encourage the lactic fermentation, put a wooden lid or china plate on the cabbage and put a weight on top of the lid. The cabbage must be soaked in its own juice, released during the packing. If the amount of juice is not sufficient, add a cold solution of boiled salted water (15 –25 g/$\frac{1}{2}$–1 oz salt to 1 litre/1$\frac{3}{4}$ pints water). Store the cabbage in an airy place. Intense fermentation begins in 3 to 5 days when the brine will bubble. It slows down then and the sauerkraut, is ready in 3–5 weeks.

Growing herbs at home
(Illustrated on page 219)

Many herbs can be grown indoors and can provide an attractive feature for a sunny window sill. Chives, parsley, basil, thyme and chervil should be sown in the spring on boxes of moist seed compost. Transfer to individual pots when large enough to handle. Cress can be grown in a shallow dish, filled with moist tissues or cotton wool. Cut the tops off celeriac or parsnip and leave in a saucer of water. The leaves will sprout in a few days and can be used as an unusual garnish or addition to salads.

Index

(Numbers in italics refer to illustrations)